SECOND CORINTHIANS

Where Life Endures

Roy L. Laurin

KREGEL PUBLICATIONS
Grand Rapids, Michigan 49501

Second Corinthians: Where Life Endures by Roy L.
Laurin
Published in 1985 by Kregel Publications,
a division of Kregel, Inc. All rights reserved.

Library of Congress Cataloging in Publication Data

Laurin, Roy L. (Roy Leonard), 1898-1966.
    2 Corinthians: Where Life Endures.

    Reprint. Originally published: II Corinthians.
3rd ed. Findlay, Ohio: Dunham Pub. Co., 1957,
c1946 (Life series of devotional expositions).
    1. Bible. N.T. Corinthians, 2nd—Commentaries.
I. Title. II. Title: Second Corinthians. III. Title:
Where life endures.
BS2675.L36   1985   227':307   85-8154
ISBN 0-8254-3129-8 (pbk.)

Printed in the United States of America

CONTENTS

SECTION I

THE ENDURANCE OF THE CHRISTIAN

II Corinthians 1-7

SECTION II

THE MINISTRATIONS OF THE CHRISTIAN

II Corinthians 8-9

SECTION III

THE COMMENDATIONS OF THE CHRISTIAN

II Corinthians 10-13

PREFACE

The studied effort in the production of this expository series is toward the devotional aspect. Technicalities and all unnecessary historical references were omitted for the sake of the practical and present application of the truth contained in the epistle.

Second Corinthians is one of the neglected Bible books, but is a mine of spiritual information and devotional inspiration.

This book is a compilation of radio addresses given on the epistle and follows the series on Romans, entitled *Life Begins* and First Corinthians, entitled *Life Matures*. Its style was developed for radio presentation but it is hoped it will be found equally profitable for devotional reading and study.

Roy L. Laurin

Pasadena, California

OUTLINE OF SECOND CORINTHIANS

CHAPTER 1

THE LIFE THAT ENDURES ADVERSITY

I. GRACE AND PEACE (verses 1-2)
II. MERCY AND COMFORT (verses 3-7)
III. DEATH AND DELIVERANCE (verses 8-11)
    A. The Danger of Paul (verse 8)
    B. The Sentence of Death (verse 9)
    C. The Deliverance of God (verse 10)
        1. "Delivered"
        2. "Doth deliver"
        3. "Will yet deliver"
    D. The Help of Prayer (verse 11)

IV. SUFFERING AND SHARING (verses 12-14)
    A. The Testimony of Conscience (verse 12)
    B. The Steadfast Confidence (verse 13)
    C. The Interrelated Christian (verse 14)

V. PURPOSE AND POSTPONEMENT (verses 15-24)
    A. Paul's Purposes (verses 17-19)
    B. God's Promises (verses 20-24)

CHAPTER 2

THE LIFE THAT ENDURES DISCIPLINE

I. JOY THROUGH GRIEF (verses 1-4)
    A. Compassion in Correction (verse 1)
    B. Joy through Correction (verse 2)
    C. Confidence by Assurance (verse 3)
    D. Love in Discipline (verse 4)

Chapter 3

THE LIFE THAT ENDURES EXPERIENCE

B. Transformation (verse 18)
1. The Beholding
2. The Changing
3. The Transforming

CHAPTER 4

THE LIFE THAT ENDURES SERVICE

I. THE PERSONAL MOTIVE (verses 1-6)
A. The Worker's Sincerity (verses 1-2)
1. Of Receiving the Gospel (verse 1)
2. Of Living the Gospel (verse 2)
B. The Unbeliever's Blindness (verses 3-4)
1. The Blind (verse 3)
2. The Blindness (verse 4)
C. The Source of Light (verses 5-6)
1. The Divine Source (verse 5)
2. The Human Source (verse 6)
II. THE VICTORIOUS SERVICE (verses 7-11)
A. The Vessel and the Treasure (verse 7)
B. The Victim and the Victory (verses 8-11)
III. THE INNER SECRET (verses 12-16)
A. The Secret of Self-Crucifixion (verse 12)
B. The Secret of Intense Faith (verse 13)
C. The Secret of a Glorious Hope (verse 14)
D. The Secret of Self-Forgetfulness (verse 15)
E. The Secret of Spiritual Strength (verse 16)
IV. THE ETERNAL REWARD (verses 17-18)
A. The Affliction and the Reward (verse 17)
1. The Present Experience
2. The Unseen Condition
3. The Future Prospect
B. The Temporal and the Eternal (verse 18)

Chapter 5

THE LIFE THAT ENDURES DYING

I. The Intermediate State of the Dead (verses 1-10)
  A. A New Body (verse 1)
  B. A New Desire (verses 2-4)
  C. A New Assurance (verse 5)
    1. This Earnest Is a Pledge
    2. This Pledge Is a Person
  D. A New Sphere (verses 6-8)
    1. It Is an Immediate State
    2. It Is a Personal State
    3. It Is a Conscious State
    4. It Is a Preferred State
  E. A New Incentive (verses 9-10)

II. The Immediate Need of the Living (verses 11-21)
  A. The New Motive in Winning Men (verses 11-15)
    1. Sincerity (verses 11-12)
    2. Unselfishness (verse 13)
    3. Love (verses 14-15)
  B. The New View of Life Which Comes to Those Won (verses 16-21)
    1. A New Creation (verses 16-17)
      a. He Is a New Creation
      b. He Lives in a New State of Life
    2. A New Ministry (verse 18)
    3. A New Message (verse 19)
    4. A New Title (verse 20)
    5. A New Condition (verse 21)
      a. Christ's Sinlessness
      b. Christ's Sinfulness
      c. Our Righteousness

Chapter 6

THE LIFE THAT ENDURES LIVING

I. Life's Relationship (verses 1-2)
   A. The Place (verse 1a)
   B. The Plea (verse 1b-2)
II. Life's Experiences (verses 3-10)
   A. Nine Testings of the Worker (verses 4-5)
      1. In Afflictions
      2. In Necessities
      3. In Distresses
      4. In Stripes
      5. In Imprisonments
      6. In Tumults
      7. In Labors
      8. In Watchings
      9. In Fastings
   B. Nine Characteristics of the Worker (verses 6-7)
      1. By Pureness
      2. By Knowledge
      3. By Long-suffering
      4. By Kindness
      5. By the Holy Ghost
      6. By Love Unfeigned
      7. By the Word of Truth
      8. By the Power of God
      9. By the Armor of Righteousness
   C. Nine Paradoxes of the Worker (verses 8-10)
      1. By Honor and Dishonor
      2. By Evil Report and Good Report
      3. As Deceivers and Yet True
      4. As Unknown and Yet Well Known
      5. As Dying and Behold We Live
      6. As Chastened and Not Killed

      7. As Sorrowful and Yet Always Rejoicing
      8. As Poor, Yet Making Many Rich
      9. As Having Nothing, and Yet Possessing All Things

III. Life's Associations (verses 11-18)
    A. The Believer's Affection for Believers (verses 11-13)
    B. The Believer's Alliance with Unbelievers (verses 14-18)
      1. "What fellowship hath righteousness with unrighteousness?"
      2. "What communion hath light with darkness?"
      3. "What concord hath Christ with Belial?"
      4. "What part hath he that believeth with an infidel?"
      5. "What argument hath the temple of God with idols?"

Chapter 7

THE LIFE THAT ENDURES CHASTENING

I. The Cleansed Life (verse 1)
    A. Negatively
      1. Filthiness of the Flesh
      2. Filthiness of the Spirit
    B. Positively

II. The Converted Life (verses 2-4)

III. The Chastened Life (verses 5-12)
    A. The Apostle's Experience with Adversity (verse 5)
    B. The Corinthians' Experience with Chastening (verses 6-12)

IV. The Comforted Life (verses 13-16)

Chapter 10

THE COMMENDATION OF CHRIST

I. The Christian's Attitude (verses 1-6)
  A. The Christian's Weapons Are Mighty
     (verse 4)
     1. In Their Contrast
     2. In Their Character
     3. In Their Conquest
II. The Christian's Authority (verses 7-11)
III. The Christian's Approval (verses 12-18)

Chapter 11

THE COMMENDATION OF SINCERITY

I. Sincerity and Service (verses 1-15)
  A. The Motives of Service (verses 1-6)
  B. The Rewards of Service (verses 7-11)
  C. The Counterfeits of Service (verses 12-15)
II. Sincerity and Suffering (verses 16-33)
  A. What They Once Were (verse 22)
  B. What They Now Are (verse 23)

Chapter 12

THE COMMENDATION OF EXPERIENCE

I. The Experience of Privilege (verses 1-6)
II. The Experience of Pain (verses 7-10)
  A. Paul's Thorn (verse 7)
  B. Pain's Source (verse 7)
  C. Pain's Purpose (verse 7)
  D. Paul's Desire (verse 8)
     1. He Asked in Prayer
     2. He Asked in Faith
     3. He Asked with Persistence

CHAPTER 13

THE COMMENDATION OF HONESTY

INTRODUCTION

It is apparent that the most practical approach to any Bible book is that which brings us at once into acquaintance with those truths which aid and help in our everyday life.

We might take the historical approach to Second Corinthians, and a certain necessity for that exists, but to consider it only in the light of the first century would never satisfy the demands of the twentieth century.

We might also take the theological approach and give its chapters a thorough theological ransacking, but this would not be entirely satisfactory. It would satisfy only a few academic souls who crave technical and abstract discussions.

Then there is the ecclesiastical approach which considers truth in the form of prejudged and preconceived molds of opinion. When it is run through these molds it has the label and features of our particular sectarian persuasions.

All of these must be rejected when we set out to consider so unusual a book as Second Corinthians. Romans contains the philosophy of Christianity. First Corinthians contains the problems of Christian churches, but Second Corinthians deals with the practice of personal Christianity. It is biographical rather than theological. It is largely the record of the Apostle Paul's personal Christianity. In this sense, Paul stands proxy for Christians of all ages. If we could forget that he was an apostle and think of him only as a disciple, his experience would stand out as a cross-section—and a composite—of all Christian experience.

The book of Second Corinthians is in no sense a systematized and orderly presentation of Christian truth. It was not conceived in the study but forged on the anvil of trial and suffering. It will therefore be found to be a record of actual life experiences rather than philosophical ideals. Here will be found a philosophy of life not so much in expressions as in experiences. The great truths that appear here are presented quite incidentally as a part of one man's life. Here "a new philosophy of life is poured forth, not through systematic treatises, but through bursts of human feeling."

Out of the maelstrom of human passions rises the figure of a real and genuine Christian. Here life is presented objectively and realistically. Here is a Christian realism that is brutally frank and meticulously honest. It is fearless to face any life situation. It is unafraid, unabashed and unashamed.

What transpires in Paul's Christian experience is the outworking of the great truths of all Christian experience. Scarcely any doctrine of the Christian faith escapes the grueling test of life's problems. Here, indeed, is life in the crucible of human experience.

The predominant word of the book is "tribulation." It traffics in the facts that have to do with the serious business of living. It can be truly said to set forth life at its worst in the world, in order to show forth life at its best in the Christian.

This book belongs, historically, to the first century, but experimentally, to the twentieth century. Let us read it and receive it as if it had been written both to us and for us.

Here we shall find that life endures. It is not endurance as dogged patience, nor is it merely the will to endure. Instead, it is a way to endure. Life endures because it has within itself the enduring life. This enduring life is the life that begins in faith and the new birth and matures under the blessings of grace. It is that phase of life which fearlessly and frankly faces current personal problems.

The Christian must be prepared for the emergencies and exigencies of life, just as any other individual. He is not miraculously protected from common troubles. Even in his most cherished position as a child of God his life has its problems. Even the privilege of prayer must be considered in this light for "when we pray for rain we must be willing to put up with some mud." We must be ready to suffer inconvenience in our own plans in order to reach the highest places in life.

Difficulties are not all pure liability. They are often necessary and beneficial even as the winnowing process is beneficial to grain and the smelting process is to precious metal. "There are defects in many characters which apparently can be removed only by some terrible experience." It is unfortunate that this is necessary, but it would be more unfortunate if it were not accomplished.

The actual writing of this epistle took place in the city of Philippi in Macedonia where Paul met Titus who had just returned from the city of Corinth with tidings concerning the church and its reaction to Paul's previous letter. So gratified was Paul with this news which Titus brought, that he sent this second letter back to Corinth with Titus as its bearer. Its purpose was twofold. It was intended to establish its author's authority as an apostle and to present to the Corinthians a practical biography of his life. Paul's authority as an apostle could be best confirmed by the genuineness of his life. This is what is set forth in this letter which is without doubt the most biographical of all Paul's writings.

The epistle divides itself into three sections which present different phases of individual Christianity.

  I. The Endurance of the Christian (chapters 1-7)
  II. The Ministrations of the Christian (chapters 8-9)
  III. The Commendations of the Christian (chapters 10-13)

A division of a book of this character must be flexible and in no sense arbitrary, because there is a total absence of sustained and progressive argument. It is filled with the expressive and sometimes explosive outbursts of its author's feelings. For this reason it does not lend itself very easily to consecutive treatment.

Section I

THE ENDURANCE OF THE CHRISTIAN

2 Corinthians 1—7

1

THE LIFE THAT ENDURES ADVERSITY

2 Corinthians 1

Life for the Christian is not a meaningless maze of unrelated events. There is a meaning and while that meaning may often be obscured, nevertheless, it is there. We do not have to understand it before it becomes true.

The life that endures adversity is set forth against a pattern of varied expression and experience.

I. GRACE AND PEACE (verses 1-2)
II. MERCY AND COMFORT (verses 3-7)
III. DEATH AND DELIVERANCE (verses 8-11)
IV. SUFFERING AND SHARING (verses 12-14)
V. PURPOSE AND POSTPONEMENT (verses 15-24)

I. GRACE AND PEACE (verses 1-2)

Paul, an apostle of Jesus Christ by the will of God, and Timothy our brother, unto the church of God which is at Corinth, with all the saints which are in all Achaia: grace be to you and peace from God our Father, and from the Lord Jesus Christ.

Here is an epistle from an apostle to the church at Corinth and the saints in Achaia. The phraseology is important. Paul was making an authoritative defense of his apostleship. He was not a religious interloper nor an ecclesiastical impostor. He was coming as an apostle of Jesus Christ. He worked as such by the will of God. His apostleship was not ecclesiastically conferred. It was not the reward of meritorious religious service. He was, as the word "apostle" means, one "sent forth." We call such a person a missionary.

This was all Paul would ever claim to be. He cared little for titles and offices. His passion was Christ and his purpose was to carry the Gospel to as many people as he could. If we would drop some of the complexities with which we are modernly encumbered and be controlled by the simplicities of early Christianity, it would make a vast difference in the effect of our Christian service.

Paul called the people saints. The title was not an artificial name given to a select few. All in Corinth and Achaia were saints.

God calls His children disciples because they are learners; believers because of their faith; saints because of their character; brethren because of their relationship; Christians because of their birth in Christ.

What an unlikely place in which to find saints! Corinth was a place of notorious immorality. It was a city of vice and impurity. It was a stronghold of paganism. Yet in the midst of that deep and wide corruption flourished a little colony of heaven. Here was a company of saints redeemed by Christ and regenerated by grace. Their lives defied human explanation. They were in Corinth, but not of it. They belonged to the society of the twice-born. They possessed the nobility of the new birth. They made an oasis of goodness in a desert of evil.

The salutation was concluded by invoking upon these people grace and peace. Grace is the cause and peace is the effect. Grace is what God gives and peace is what we receive. Peace will be in proportion to the grace we appropriate.

II. Mercy and Comfort (verses 3-7)

Blessed be God, even the Father of our Lord Jesus Christ, the Father of mercies, and the God of all comfort; who comforteth us in all our tribulation, that we may be able to comfort them which are in any trouble, by the comfort wherewith we ourselves are comforted of God. For as the sufferings of Christ abound in us, so our consolation also aboundeth by Christ. And whether we be afflicted, it is for your consolation and salvation, which is effectual in the enduring of the same sufferings which we also suffer: or whether we be comforted, it is for your consolation and salvation. And our hope of you is stedfast, knowing, that as ye are partakers of the sufferings, so shall ye be also of·the consolation.

Here the two greatest human needs are met by the two greatest divine provisions. Man is born a sinner and a sorrower. He needs mercy for his sins and comfort for his sorrow.

For man's sins God provides mercy. We who deserve justice are shown mercy. As David said: ''He hath not dealt with us after our sins; nor rewarded us according to our iniquities. For as the heaven is high above the earth, so great is his mercy toward them that fear him'' (Psalm 103:10-11).

God ministers mercy for our sins through His Son. This is done historically by the Cross where ''He is the propitiation for our sins'' and experimentally, by regeneration.

For man's sorrow God provides comfort. There is no exemption from sorrow, and there is no exception in God's comfort. He is the God of ''all comfort.''

Comfort is more than condolence and consolation. It is more than sympathy that soothes our torn and bleeding hearts. Comfort as used here comes from a word which means ''a paraclete'' or ''one called alongside.'' Jesus said: ''I will not leave you comfortless.'' In that instance He literally said: ''I will not leave you orphans.'' In His place would come another, the blessed Comforter who is the Holy Spirit. Thus the entire Trinity is at one time or another designated as the Comforter. Comfort is the help of a divine person who comes to our side in the extremity of our sorrow and affliction.

This help is of the nature of inner peace. It is more

than pious assistance. God, the one called alongside to help, bolsters the soul and strengthens the foundations. He rock-ribs the footings of life. He provides the balm of Gilead. And, in the midst of falling tears and a broken heart, we can say: "I will magnify the Lord."

The comfort of God is not only a variety of blessing, but it is by various means.

In one case it is the comfort of God's Word: "Wherefore comfort one another with these words." In another case it is the comfort of God's love. Then it may be the comfort of Christ's presence, for He said: "I will never leave thee, nor forsake thee." Again it is the comfort of Christ's resurrection. Together with all these it is also the comfort of Christ's coming. These combine to be the ministry of God's comfort for our sorrow.

The remedy for sin and sorrow is found in Christ's redemption. Sin was met by crucifixion. Sorrow was met by resurrection. Both remedies remain as historical provisions until our faith lays hold of them in a personal acceptance and experience of Christ.

There must be a point of contact between our sin and sorrow and God's mercy and comfort. The meeting place is faith and the new birth. Mercy is not the consequence of our good intentions any more than comfort is the consequence of our yearnings. We must establish a point of contact with God. It must be life on a new basis. When our faith reaches out to embrace God's Son the place of contact is reached and the flow of mercy and comfort begins like the water that gushes from an artesian well.

Why should we seek comfort for our sorrow? Is its highest good what it does for us in soothing our feelings? No, the motive should be the purpose of God, for God has a purpose in imparting comfort. It is expressed in the fourth verse: "Who comforteth us in all our tribulation, that we may be able to comfort them which are in any trouble, by the comfort wherewith we ourselves are comforted of God." Arthur S. Way's translation begins the verse by saying: "Blessed be He who in all my affliction comforts me so perfectly that I have comfort to spare." It is this "comfort to spare" which is God's purpose in comforting us and our motive in receiving comfort. The comfort which comes to us "in all our tribulation" is intended as spiritual equipment through experience that we who have been comforted may "be able to comfort them which are in any trouble." And the means by which we are to comfort is the same means by which we have been comforted.

It may not be all the truth to say that we cannot comfort unless we ourselves have known sorrow, but it is certainly true that we cannot feel another's sorrow until we have felt the sting of pain. Neither can we ever know the sweetness of comfort until we have felt the soothing touch of God's love in a broken heart.

"Great hearts can only be made by great troubles. The spade of trouble digs the reservoir of comfort deeper, and makes more room for the water of consolation."

The Psalms of David are the sweetest words of comfort because his pen had been dipped in the ink of affliction.

Whoever will feel the keenest and serve the best must have his feelings hurt the most.

There is altogether too little of the ministry of comfort. Too many Christians are busy these days in the disgraceful orgy of criticizing instead of the blessed ministry of comforting. Instead of calming troubled waters, they are stirring them up. Instead of going about in the Master's Name soothing and comforting, they are cutting and hurting.

It is so easy to seek comfort and so difficult to give it. Most of us want sympathy and kindness for our own troubles and are gravely offended if we are neglected. So few seek out the broken hearts of men that they might reproduce in these the comfort God has produced in them.

Have you been comforted? It is an obligation for you then to be a comforter. Has God come alongside to help you in an hour of calamity? It is required of you then to be a companion to another in his hour of calamity. Begin today to do what you have neglected for so long. Begin at home and then extend your ministrations as far as strength and time permit.

This kind of ministry does not require wealth or education. All it requires is the experience of God's comfort. All it takes is the understanding of a broken heart and the wealth of divine love. If you have these things, you have all you need to perform a great service.

As Christ's sufferings overflow in us we shall discover that our consolation will overflow by Christ through us. We shall prove to be a channel of overflowing consolation to a sorrowing world. Dare we believe that and consider our own immediate sufferings as the lessons of life for the ministry of comfort? Dare we extend ourselves in an honest effort to alleviate the pain of the sufferer, the lonesomeness of the invalid, the helplessness of the cripple, the tears of the sorrower and the grief of the sinner?

The "sufferings of Christ" are not to be construed as a continuation of His atoning work on the Cross. He plainly said that was finished. The sufferings of the Cross were once for all. They cannot be repeated. Neither Paul nor we can reproduce Christ's suffering for any atoning purpose, but since Christ suffered for us we are to bear the sufferings of others. Christ took our sufferings that we might take others' sufferings. This gives a new pattern to life. It is not a selfish religious ceremonialism, but a real and vicarious Christianity. The Hindu prostrates his form in the dust or walks on spikes or burns his flesh in order to suffer for self-salvation, whereas in Christianity, the Christian enters into the sufferings of Christ that he may bear the sufferings of others.

In the book *Quo Vadis* it is recorded, and this is only legend, that as Peter fled from burning Rome and its multitudes of martyred Christians, he was met on the Appian Way by Jesus. Peter called out: "Quo vadis" —"Lord, whither goest Thou?" Jesus replied: "I go to Rome." Immediately Peter knew his place was in Rome with Jesus who was going there to stand beside His dying and suffering disciples.

In this day of increased tragedy—not just extraordinary tragedy but common tragedy when men and women are suffering more of the common sorrows and pains of life—our place is among the sufferers. No disciples of Christ dare flee their modern Romes for selfish isolation. None dare live in castles of carefreeness while the whole world burns to the tune of evil fiddlers. We who say "Quo vadis" must cease our fleeing and follow Christ back to the place of sorrow.

Paul wanted the brethren at Corinth to know that he had been in great peril. He was the object of satanic hatred. His life was a constant battle against adverse forces and circumstances. This letter of biography speaks of fears within and foes without.

It is the nature of Christianity to thrive on adversity. Christianity was born and grew up in the midst of persecution. Let none of us entertain the notion that we are to be free from it.

III. DEATH AND DELIVERANCE (verses 8-11)

We find four things set forth in this hazardous experience of Paul.

A. *The Danger of Paul* (verse 8)

For we would not, brethren, have you ignorant of our trouble which came to us in Asia, that we were pressed out of measure, above strength, insomuch that we despaired even of life.

Whatever this danger was, is a matter of conjecture. The important thing is not what it was, but what it produced.

What Paul was anxious to convey to his Corinthian friends was the reality of his predicament. Apparently some were discounting Paul's problems and saying that his life was sheltered and soft.

We notice particularly the apostle's reaction to his difficulty. He was no braggart who boasted of his own great conquests. He frankly admitted his fear. He told how depressed he was and how he gave up hope of surviving. His reactions were as normal as ours and his experiences were as common as ours though undoubtedly greatly increased and intensified.

A workman was employed on a building project where it was necessary for him to work at night. While busy on the edge of a wall several stories high, he lost his balance and in his fall managed to grasp the edge of the wall with his hands. He clung desperately, hoping that someone would hear his call and rescue him. It was completely dark and the noise of riveting machines and a myriad of mechanical sounds drowned out his cries for help. Gradually his arms grew numb and his strength gave out. Slowly his fingers slipped, against every effort of his will to hold on, and at last he lost his hold and with a terrifying cry fell—about three inches— to a scaffold that had been there all the time. The darkness prevented his seeing it and all through his anxiety he was safe.

This is like many of our experiences. We are terrified by our predicament while all the time there is the scaffold of God's care beneath us. Our ignorance does not change its certainty although it does destroy our peace. Sight does not see what only faith can apprehend, that "underneath are the everlasting arms."

B.   *The Sentence of Death* (verse 9)

But we had the sentence of death in ourselves, that we should not trust in ourselves, but in God which raiseth the dead.

When Paul surveyed his situation and asked himself what the end would be, he had to sentence himself to death. It was futile to trust in himself. It was impossible to find adequate human aid. Paul was beyond help from man. But he still had God and he found a new trust in God. It taught him to rely no more on his own strength but in God who can raise from the dead.

Here was faith born of failure. Here was a new confidence in God. Out of a bitter experience that was so perilous that it almost took his life, Paul found a new faith. These experiences either leave us better or worse. We either have more faith or are more fearful. Either we are mellowed or we are embittered.

C.   *The Deliverance of God* (verse 10)

Who delivered us from so great a death, and doth deliver: in whom we trust that he will yet deliver us.

The threefold deliverance referred to was a deliverance associated with Paul's personal problem. The conviction expressed was born out of the experience he had lately passed through, in which God had miraculously saved his life.

Do we have convictions born of experience, or is our Christian faith a theoretical summary of ideas? So many people believe God only in their ideas. They do not know God in their lives. God is far-off and distant. Here is the recital of a personal and individual Christianity which should belong to all. Let us bring our Christianity down out of our heads and make it motivate our hands and feet. After all, it is a life for service and a way to walk.

Paul spoke of deliverance in three tenses.

    1. ''Delivered.''

This is past tense and it is the deliverance he referred to in a previous verse.

    2. ''Doth deliver.''

This is the present tense and takes Christianity out of the realm of reminiscence and memory and makes it a matter of the present. Too much of our Christianity is in the past tense. We relate our experiences of yesterday without any freshness. Bring your experience down to date. Take it out of yesterday and put it into today.

    3. ''Will yet deliver.''

This is the future tense and makes deliverance a continuing quality. We have something in prospect. Too many have their experiences only in retrospect. We should be looking ahead and not behind. There is great danger of elderly Christians living only in the past. Look ahead! Turn your face toward the future. God is there as well as in the past. What He has been is the assurance of what He will be. God is not an experiment for a true Christian. He is an experience. Do not fret about the impending disaster. Think only of the immanent God. The best is not past. It is to come. We talk too much about ''the good old days'' when we ought to anticipate the glorious days that are coming.

D. *The Help of Prayer* (verse 11)

Ye also helping together by prayer for us, that for the gift bestowed upon us by the means of many persons thanks may be given by many on our behalf.

By this statement Paul established the connection which one Christian's prayers have to another Christian's need. It is the vital connection of aid and assistance. Called here ''helping together by prayer,'' it is an effectual and necessary means of assistance which we render each other.

The effect of prayer accrues not only to the benefit of the one prayed for, but results in blessing to the one who prays. It is God's intention that the joy of achievement should be proportionate. Paul did not think of himself as one to consume all the credit and take all the glory. The success of Paul's great ministry and miraculous preservation of life in the midst of many dangers was to be shared by many and not just by one. Deliverance was granted Paul ''by the means of many persons.''

IV. SUFFERING AND SHARING (verses 12-14)

Let us look at three things in these verses.

A. *The Testimony of Conscience* (verse 12)

For our rejoicing is this, the testimony of our conscience, that in simplicity and godly sincerity, not with fleshly wisdom, but by the grace of God, we have had our conversation in the world, and more abundantly to you-ward.

Paul was referring to his relation, as a Christian minister, to the world and to the church. He had been charged with insincerity by certain enemies at Corinth. They wrote letters that impugned his character. Against these unjust accusations Paul defended himself. Sometimes a servant of Christ can defend himself and should, not for his own carnal satisfaction but for the sake of his ministry. However, many times he can only suffer in silence, awaiting the vindication God will bring.

Paul found an opportunity here to speak in behalf of himself. The testimony of his conscience was "simplicity and godly sincerity." His ministry was not embellished with personal pursuits. It was not garish and covetous. It was not pretense or sham.

Paul's character and career were his best defense. He did not need defenders or votes of confidence. He stood on his own feet and those feet were planted solidly on his own record.

B. *The Steadfast Confidence* (verse 13)

For we write none other things unto you, than what ye read or acknowledge; and I trust ye shall acknowledge even to the end.

Paul sought the continuing confidence of his Corinthian friends who were being misled by personal enemies who were trying to turn them away from their early confidence in Paul.

C. *The Interrelated Christian* (verse 14)

As also ye have acknowledged us in part, that we are your rejoicing, even as ye also are our's in the day of the Lord Jesus.

The verse is summed up in a few words. "We are your rejoicing even as ye also are our's." Here is an interrelation of Christians which reveals the importance of confidence in each other and steadfastness to each other.

Paul could not get along without them and they could not get along without him. There is a sense in which we do not need the approval of our brethren for, "If God be for us, who can be against us?" But if the pattern of unity and the harmony of the body is to be preserved and kept intact, the confident and ultimate relation which one believer has to another must be preserved.

Paul finally put before them the great adjustment day of the Judgment Seat of Christ. Then the work of these saboteurs of character would come to light.

Then those who had lent themselves to the petty things of gossip and talebearing which divided brethren, would be exposed. Let us be big and noble and Christlike so that the review of our lives by the scrutiny of Christ will cause rejoicing instead of regret.

V. Purpose and Postponement (verses 15-24)

The purpose of Paul to visit Corinth is expressed in verses 15-16:

And in this confidence I was minded to come unto you before, that ye might have a second benefit; and to pass by you into Macedonia, and to come again out of Macedonia unto you, and of you to be brought on my way toward Judaea.

The instance referred to was Paul's expressed intention to make a trip to Corinth. His intention was to take the sea route to Macedonia by way of Corinth, but his plans miscarried, for Paul was subject to divine call and direction. Because the plans miscarried a few saboteurs at Corinth, who were like vultures in character, used this chance to attack him. They said he never intended to come in the first place. They accused him of being afraid. They suspected his motives and attacked his character. They said he was neither a man of his word nor a man of honor.

When Paul was obliged to change his plans and postpone his purpose it was neither a mark of weakness nor an evidence of dishonesty. Any right-minded and Christ-minded Christian will agree that purposes of the most inviolate kind are subject to postponement. No one, be he the most sincere Christian, can always foresee every circumstance nor always predetermine every detail of the will of God.

Probably every servant of Christ has found himself in some such predicament as Paul did. He may have earnestly and sincerely declared intentions which circumstances or further enlightenment, as to the will

of God, forbade him fulfilling. An expressed intention may need to be changed and if it is changed, it is
not necessarily a sign of fickleness or a lack of personal integrity.

What applies to apostles in this case, is for disciples
as well. The principle of independence of action as
well as independence of conscience belongs to every
Christian, whether apostle or disciple, minister or lay-
man. If you feel led to postpone a purpose and change
a course, do it. It may not meet with the approval of
others, but so long as you are right before God and
right with yourself, you can afford to be wrong to everyone else.

After all, our lives do not always follow a straight
course. The Apostle Paul had to change his plans
many times. He had purposed to visit the church at
Rome many times but in the providence of God his purpose was postponed.

Sailboats in a race have a prescribed course laid out
for them from starting point to finishing line, but they
do not go in a straight line toward the goal. They follow a sailor's strategy of tacking, in order to take advantage of the wind. If they sailed their craft on a
straight course, they would be becalmed and lose the
race. Let us, too, take advantage of new and fuller
light and advantageous and providential circumstances. Let us keep our eyes on the goal and our
hand on the tiller and resolutely sail ahead.

We notice that Paul did not stop his work to contend
with his enemies. He kept on toward the goal.

The Cleveland *Plain Dealer* printed an editorial
some years ago that is very helpful.

"If I had to stop my work every time anyone shot at me, I
would never get anything done." So Colonel Roosevelt, in the
Spanish-American War, is reported to have answered a solicitous
officer who wanted him to move his tent to a place better sheltered
from the enemy's fire.

And so the people who get things done have had to think and answer since the world began. For almost everybody is the target for some kind of shot, and the more ambitious one may be, the more numerous the attacks. To turn about, or try to dodge or answer them, only leads one away from his main purpose. Some people get so busy answering criticism that they forget what they started out to do.

Then there are those who seem to spend their whole lives looking for slights or imagining snubs or grieving when they get them, for, of course, they get what they are looking for. Such people never have had any absorbing interest in life to begin with. If they could have engrossing work or interest, they would be surprised to find that there were no more slights, for they would not have time to think about them, and a slight is not a slight unless there is a mind ready to receive it.

It was Spurgeon who told us of two little boys, one a very bad little boy and the other a very good little boy. The bad little boy went out to throw mud at the moon and the good little boy took a basin of water and went to wash it off. But, what do you suppose the moon was doing all the time? Just shining on as usual and shedding its light over the darkened earth while the little boys were throwing mud and splashing water.

Two things are thrown into contrast.

A. *Paul's Purposes* (verses 17-19)

When I therefore was thus minded, did I use lightness? or the things that I purpose, do I purpose according to the flesh, that with me there should be yea yea, and nay nay? But as God is true, our word toward you was not yea and nay. For the Son of God, Jesus Christ, who was preached among you by us, even by me and Silvanus and Timotheus, was not yea and nay, but in him was yea.

Paul declared his purposes to be those of a sincere and forthright Christian. He was not a shifty opportunist who played politics with the interests and welfare of others. He did not say one thing and mean another.

Paul dared to substantiate the quality of his character by the nature of his preaching. The Gospel he preached was reliable and positive. So was the preacher of that Gospel. Happy the man who can measure his character by his preaching. Paul could and he stood justified.

B. *God's Promises* (verses 20-24)

For all the promises of God in him are yea, and in him Amen, unto the glory of God by us. Now he which stablisheth us with you in Christ, and hath anointed us, is God; who hath also sealed us, and given the earnest of the Spirit in our hearts. Moreover I call God for a record upon my soul, that to spare you I came not as yet unto Corinth. Not for that we have dominion over your faith, but are helpers of your joy: for by faith ye stand.

Paul called attention to the stability of the promises of God. It was this stability which had produced in Paul the straightforwardness of his life.

God's promises are affirmed by His will and sealed by His Amen. Do we ever ask if God's promises will all be fulfilled? The certainty of their fulfillment is sealed in the very character of God. Circumstances will not change God's plans, though they may change ours. Postponement may alter our purposes, but never defer God's faithfulness. The certainty and assurance of this are to be found in the indwelling Holy Spirit.

The Holy Spirit is set forth as a Seal—"who hath . . . sealed us." A seal was a mark or a sign of ownership. It was engraved with the owner's likeness and when placed on documents, which were usually written on soft clay, it left its mark as an assurance of safety. It is in this sense that we have been sealed by the Holy Spirit with Christ's image impressed upon us.

The Holy Spirit is also set forth as an Earnest—"and given the earnest of the Spirit in our hearts." This referred to an advance payment that guaranteed and assured possession until the day of complete and final redemption. In this way property was bought by placing the earnest money as a pledge of full payment. In the same way the indwelling Spirit is the pledge of our final and complete redemption.

2

THE LIFE THAT ENDURES DISCIPLINE

2 Corinthians 2

This explanation of the personal feelings of the Apostle Paul reveals his Christian humility. It is revealed to us here that it might be reflected through us elsewhere. After all, the purpose of these intimate touches of biography is not merely to record incidental matters belonging to the first century. Their practice belongs to our century and to us who face the responsibility of being Christians in fact as well as in faith.

This chapter falls into three self-evident sections.

    I. Joy Through Grief (verses 1-4)
    II. Restoration Through Forgiveness (verses 5-11)
    III. Triumph Through Christ (verses 12-17)

I. Joy Through Grief (verses 1-4)

These verses deal with the apostle's experience in a pastoral capacity. He had just finished saying in the last verse of the previous chapter that he did not want to have dominion over their faith. He was not craving authority in other people's affairs. He sought only to be a help. Such help as he could render he would be glad to render at the expense of his own comfort and even his own reputation.

In these things Paul stands as an example of an ideal Christian pastor. The ideal is not an ecclesiastical autocrat, nor is he a religious hireling who performs a duty. It is not essential that he excels in the intellectual presentation of truth. All of these, leadership, dutifulness and preaching, are required of pastors, but these alone are not enough. Pastors are to be fellow sufferers and fellow sharers with their flock. They are to feel sorrow and joy. They are to suffer in sympathy. They are to be prayerful in counsel. They are to feel the pulse of human passion and enter into the affairs of their people. They are to stand before them to preach truth and to walk with them in order to practice that truth.

Paul reveals the pastor's heart and life in the following aspects.

A. *Compassion in Correction* (verse 1)

But I determined this with myself, that I would not come again to you in heaviness.

He was so tenderly mindful of their feelings that he deferred his visit so as not to cause further distress. He realized that a visit at the time intended would have been an occasion for severe disciplinary measures. He hoped to avoid disciplining them, not that they might prolong their abuses, but that they might have time to correct them of their own volition. There was genuine compassion in Paul's correction. There ought to be in all correction. To inflict a wound of discipline without providing a salve of healing may be punitive, but it certainly is not corrective.

B. *Joy Through Correction* (verse 2)

For if I make you sorry, who is he then that maketh me glad, but the same which is made sorry by me?

These people were Paul's source of joy. If he prolonged their sorrow, they could not be a joy to him. He told them that his joy was not in coming to them with the rod of correction. He would rather feed them than punish them.

We must not lose sight of the fact that Paul had dealt severely with these people. He had not been unwilling to administer rebuke and correction. He had been faithful, but his great joy would have been in seeing these same people blossoming in the radiance and fragrance of a happy Christian experience.

C. *Confidence by Assurance* (verse 3)

And I wrote this same unto you, lest, when I came, I should have sorrow from them of whom I ought to rejoice; having confidence in you all, that my joy is the joy of you all.

Paul's confidence in these Corinthian Christians was the assurance that they would correct these abuses and Christian irregularities before he came. He expressed himself as feeling confident that since the wrongs of their lives had been brought to their attention they would see the need of correction and immediately attend to it.

Here is a quality of friendship that lacks suspicion. It attributes high motives and anticipates the best results. It is seen to its best advantage when displayed in a pastor's ministrations to his people.

How eagerly Paul craved the spiritual advancement of his Christian friends at Corinth is seen in this outburst of expressive feeling. "I wrote this same unto you, lest, when I came, I should have sorrow from them of whom I ought to rejoice."

D. *Love in Discipline* (verse 4)

For out of much affliction and anguish of heart I wrote unto you with many tears; not that ye should be grieved, but that ye might know the love which I have more abundantly unto you.

The crowning concern of Paul's pastor-heart was that they "might know the love which I have more abundantly unto you." In all the harsh measures he had to employ, the prompting purpose was love. He loved them; therefore, he hurt them. The greatest proof of love is not pampering, but discipline.

Discipline reveals the true depths of a father's heart. What father ever delights in disciplining his child? No father with a true heart. He is torn with anguish at every stroke of the rod. He would a thousand times prefer it himself. But he is faithful in his duty, because he knows that the fruits of chastisement are sweet and wholesome.

Therein lies the hidden idea of blessing out of pain and joy out of grief. The greatest blessings and the fullest joys are sometimes those which are distilled from the deepest sorrows. The greatest affections sometimes come from the strictest discipline.

The greatest problem of a pastor is not to be found in his study but in his parish. The day may come when his motives will be called into question, when slander will be heaped upon him and when lies and misunderstandings will multiply. What should he do in a situation of that kind? The course he should follow is suggested in the following particulars.

II. Restoration Through Forgiveness (verses 5-11)

A. *The Offender's Greater Grief* (verses 5-6)

But if any have caused grief, he hath not grieved me, but in part: that I may not overcharge you all. Sufficient to such a man is this punishment, which was inflicted of many.

Apparently, the offense was against Paul personally. This seems likely to refer to some insult or affront suffered by Paul at the hands of some backslidden saboteur of character. The motive of the offense was not given, but it can be easily imagined from the practical experience of a modern servant. He is subjected to all sorts of attacks. Many times they are of his own making, but not so in the case of Paul who was the innocent victim of a vicious and violent offender.

Paul had been frank to state the facts in previous instances of open calumniation, but he never went to the lengths of seeking personal vindication and retribution.

We must expect inconsistencies and injustices. So long as there are carnal and imperfect Christians, there will always be inconsistent Christianity. Being reconciled to this fact, we must be determined to stand up to it with the spirit of Jesus Christ. Jesus' method was not to fight fire with fire, but to conquer hatred with love and abuse with affection.

Since we are partakers of the divine nature we will normally reveal the character of that nature in our relations in life.

Someone asked Sadhu Sundar Singh, the late remarkable Christian mystic, if he understood the meaning of perfect love of which John speaks. The Sadhu smiled and quietly said: "When I throw a stone at a fruit tree, the fruit tree throws not a stone back, but gives me fruit. Is it that?" Then he asked: "Should not we who love the Lord Jesus, be like sandalwood which imparts its fragrance to the axe which cuts it?"

The apostle's attitude toward the offender was that he had the greater grief. The injury he had inflicted on himself was far greater than that inflicted upon Paul. He who wrongs another, damages himself far more than the other. He will shrivel his soul and put the acid of bitterness into his affections and dam up the springs of his faith. It is far worse to injure than to be injured.

This man, however, had not been permitted to go unchallenged. He had been censured. But the censure was not Paul's personal abuse. It was the censure of the church as the constituted body of Christ with His authority to institute disciplinary measures. It was the punishment of church discipline. Such discipline had been carried out in the order set forth in the Christian principles of church government.

We notice how democratic this procedure was. It was democracy saturated with theocracy. It was spirit-filled believers fulfilling, with a complete absence of ecclesiastical autocracy, the leadership God had given them.

B. *The Forgiveness of Brethren* (verses 7-8)

So that contrariwise ye ought rather to forgive him, and comfort him, lest perhaps such a one should be swallowed up with overmuch sorrow. Wherefore I beseech you that ye would confirm your love toward him.

The motive in forgiveness is the complete restoration of the penitent offender. Penitence is required of the offender before forgiveness is required of the offended. But more than this is required. In this case forgiveness was required of those who sympathized with the one offended. Many times the offended person, who may have been injured very grievously, is quicker to forgive than those who sympathize with him.

Forgiveness is more than a feeling. It should be motivated by a desire to see the penitent offender restored to a place of useful fellowship. It should be inspired with a passion to spare the guilty person from an overwhelming grief and sorrow. And so Paul suggests that we forgive "lest perhaps such a one should be swallowed up with overmuch sorrow."

We can test the sincerity of our faith and the earnestness of our own convictions by the attitude we have toward those who transgress the peace and purity of God's people. If we gloat over their fall and rejoice in their censure, we have revealed ourselves as coming far short of the Christian ideal. Paul called upon the Corinthians to "confirm" their love by the forgiveness of restoration. The word "confirm" means "validity." They were to show the validity of their love by the grace of forgiveness.

C. *The Purpose of Paul* (verses 9-11)

For to this end also did I write, that I might know the proof of you, whether ye be obedient in all things. To whom ye forgive any thing, I forgive also: for if I forgave any thing, to whom I

forgave it, for your sakes forgave I it in the person of Christ; lest
Satan should get an advantage of us: for we are not ignorant of
his devices.

The purpose of Paul was to inspire forgiveness and
to require obedience. He had written to test their loyalty to him. He had found them obedient and faithful.
He had also written to inspire forgiveness, but he was
not requiring what he was not willing to do himself. He
had first forgiven the offender in his own heart. Now
he sought to see forgiveness in the lives of his friends.

More than this, it was something done as in the very
sight of Christ. The phrase "in the person of Christ"
as used in verse 10 literally means "in the presence of
Christ." Paul was not acting for Christ in a priestly
and mediatorial capacity. He was acting in Christ. He
was not acting as Christ, but instead with Christ. He was
acting in the Spirit of Christ rather than in the place of
Christ. None of us can ever take the place of Christ,
but we can act in such a way as to multiply Him in daily
life.

Paul advised all this because of a great concern. He
says that we should observe all the foregoing, "Lest
Satan should get an advantage of us: for we are not ignorant of his devices."

Paul knew and understood the strategy of Satan in
his diabolical work in the flock of God. Satan first seeks
to get Christians to overlook sin, fail to discipline it and
condone the offender. Then he seeks to establish the
other extreme. If discipline is meted out, he seeks to
harden the Christian against the offender and refuse to
take him back when penitent. It is as much a sin to keep
him out when he repents as it is to keep him in when he
persists in willful and known sin.

The Bible is not without careful instruction to the
shepherds of God's flock. It would be strange indeed if
it gave teaching for the sheep and no instruction for the

shepherd. It would be a mark of incompleteness and a
lack of foresight, but the Bible does not lack in this respect. In the next verses we find important ideals for
the Christian pastor. Paul has turned from the personal
trials of the pastor to the triumph which he may enjoy
as he observes the ideals which are set forth.

III. Triumph Through Christ (verses 12-17)

All of the subject matter of these verses revolves upon
the personal experience of Paul and his pastoral care
for the Corinthians as well as his own ideals as a servant
of Christ.

A. *A Pastor's Concern* (verses 12-13)

Furthermore, when I came to Troas to preach Christ's gospel,
and a door was opened unto me of the Lord, I had no rest in my
spirit, because I found not Titus my brother: but taking my leave
of them, I went from thence into Macedonia.

Paul had reached another open door of opportunity.
It was at a place called "The Troad" because of its
proximity to ancient Troy. He was greatly troubled
upon reaching this field of service because Titus had
not returned there from Corinth. So agitated was he
at this disappointment that he left without completing
his mission. He went on to Macedonia where he apparently hoped to meet Titus.

No minister of Christ can be at his best while concerned over the continued failures of his people. Paul
was so upset and so concerned that he failed to enter the
open door at Troas. It is a solemn reflection when we
consider how often quarreling Christians have hindered
God's work because they put an intolerable burden on
God's worker. Time spent in nourishing the feelings of
a broken heart and in efforts to compose quarrels among
God's people is time lost for eternity. It might otherwise have been used in entering some open door.

B. *A Pastor's Triumph* (verse 14)

Now thanks be unto God, which always causeth us to triumph in Christ, and maketh manifest the savour of his knowledge by us in every place.

Way's rendering of this verse is so suggestive. It reads: "Now, thank God, it is He who everywhere leads me, leads me in Messiah's triumph procession. By me He wafts abroad through every land the knowledge of Jesus, the incense of His triumphal march."

This is a description of a Christian version of a Roman triumphal procession. In Paul's day public honor was bestowed upon a victorious commander by vote of the senate. It was the greatest possible reward any one could receive. The honor was a march of triumph through the city of Rome. The march of triumph moved through the streets to the national temple where sacrifices were offered to Jupiter.

The procession included victors and victims. The victors, with the commander at the head, were followed by the conquered army including the vanquished king, officers and soldiers who were dragged by chains fastened to the chariots of the victors and were led off to a life of captivity. Long lines of captives bore censers filled with burning incense. Sweet spices and aromatics were strewn upon the street and everywhere was the scented fragrance of victory's perfume. It was a notable occasion and an unforgettable sight.

Such will be the triumph of one who follows Christ as Paul did. Christ will lead to triumph. No matter what the adversities or adversaries, the end will be the triumphant procession of Christian victory.

C. *A Pastor's Influence* (verses 15-16)

For we are unto God a sweet savour of Christ, in them that are saved, and in them that perish: to the one we are the savour of death unto death; and to the other the savour of life unto life. And who is sufficient for these things?

The triumph spoken of in the previous verse is not only an anticipation; it is an experience. Every true minister and each humble disciple is a censer of incense, wafting the fragrance of Christ upon an ill-smelling civilization. In a world which has become a charnel house, we may bring the incense of a beautiful fragrance. In homes and in hearts of sorrow and sin, we may waft abroad the incense of Christ's triumphal march. Wherever men take Christ in this dark world, there is being scattered the sweet smell of redemption. We may be wafters of such perfume as this in our day and in our places.

Seneca said: "He who frequents the perfumer's shop and lingers even for a short time, will carry with him the scent of the place."

What does it mean when it says that we are "the savour of death unto death; and to the other the savour of life unto life"? As we march on with Christ the Gospel has a twofold effect. In some it convicts and converts to life, while in others it confirms their death. To those already dead in sin its refusal confirms the inherent state of death. But to those who believe and join this procession of triumph, it becomes the fragrance of life.

The sun, shining upon a tree, brings life to some branches and death to others. If a branch is vitally connected to the tree and the tree is properly rooted in the soil, the sun brings life. On the other hand, if a branch has been broken off, the sun will wither and scorch it to death. The same sun is a savor of life unto life and a savor of death unto death. So is the Gospel. If we put ourselves in right relation to it through faith, it brings life, but if we refuse that relation through unbelief, it brings death.

D. *A Pastor's Preaching* (verse 17)

For we are not as many, which corrupt the word of God: but as of sincerity, but as of God, in the sight of God speak we in Christ.

In its original sense the expression Paul used refers to a vintner or wine merchant who deals in corrupt trading practices by diluting his wine and selling it as a pure product. There are false teachers who are like that. They are men who seek to make a personal profit from divine things. Like dishonest merchants, they mix the wine of truth to gain a selfish advantage. They adulterate the truth and are fraudulent hucksters of God's message.

One word characterized Paul's preaching and it should dominate ours—"sincerity." It is more to be desired than oratory, brilliance, education and personal prominence. To be honorable, sincere and spiritually wholesome in dealing with divine truth and in living the Christian life, is more becoming to Christ's servant than any other attribute in the category of virtue.

God give us a generation of such men!

3

THE LIFE THAT ENDURES EXPERIENCE
2 Corinthians 3

In Paul's biography appear valuable lessons for every Christian. There is presented to us in a very specific sense the motives of personal Christian experience. Christians are born but they are not born matured or adult. They must grow and develop spiritually.

Most of us have had the idea that birds fly naturally, but such is not the case. Flying is a difficult and complicated process, even to a bird. It is born to be a flier, yet it must learn how to fly. A bird must learn how to use air currents for soaring. It must understand how to angle for air with its wings and must know how to bank, power-dive, roll, take off, zoom and land in relation to the wind. It must learn how to use its wings as man learns how to use his feet.

For centuries falconers have known that a bird flown during the middle of the day will soar away and never return. Just why this was could never be understood until airplane pilots discovered that at noon, warm, rising air currents make it difficult to land a plane. A bird trying to land will get caught in these rising currents and will find it almost impossible to return to its master.

These things are a matter of learning and experience. What is true in the natural realm has its counterpart in the spiritual. Christians must learn to live the ideals of the new nature born within them in the new birth.

Here are exploited the motives in the Christian's personal life.

I. THE CHRISTIAN'S QUALIFICATIONS (verses 1-6)
II. THE CHRISTIAN'S INSPIRATION (verses 7-11)
III. THE CHRISTIAN'S TRANSFORMATION (verses 12-18)

I. THE CHRISTIAN'S QUALIFICATIONS (verses 1-6)

Paul presented three possible qualifications, one of which he summarily rejected. Then he allowed himself to stand or fall on the basis of the other two sources of justification of both himself and his ministry.

A. *The Personal Qualification* (verse 1)

Do we begin again to commend ourselves? or need we, as some others, epistles of commendation to you, or letters of commendation from you?

When it came to credentials of both character and career Paul found it not only unnecessary but unwise to justify himself. He found it totally unnecessary to commend himself by a lengthy defense of his motives and his record.

He also found it unnecessary to build a good opinion of himself on the letters he could receive from others. Letters of recommendation are not always sincere. A person's best credentials are not what people say about him but what they see in him.

Of course, letters of introduction and credentials have their place, but they can never take the place of personal performance. Let us learn to live and act so that our Christian character is self-evident, and then our record will be our best recommendation.

B. *The Corinthian Qualification* (verses 2-3)

For eloquent credentials Paul could refer to the Corinthians and say, "You are my credentials." They were his letter of recommendation. He called them such when he said: "Ye are our epistle."

The credentials dealt with here are twofold.

1. The Corinthians Were Paul's Credential (verse 2)

Ye are our epistle written in our hearts, known and read of all men.

There were those who had been insinuating that Paul was not a divinely accredited apostle. These detractors contended that Paul should present letters of credentials to substantiate his claims. Paul countered their argument and accusation by saying that the proof of his genuineness was to be found in his converts at Corinth. They were his credentials. Before they had been pagans; now they were Christians. The change in their lives was a divine one and Paul was the instrument. These converts were the seal of divine approval upon Paul's ministry.

2. The Christians Are Christ's Credential (verse 3)

Forasmuch as ye are manifestly declared to be the epistle of Christ ministered by us, written not with ink, but with the Spirit of the living God; not in tables of stone, but in fleshy tables of the heart.

The changed lives of Christians constitute the best possible proof of the reality of Christianity. Wherever the message of Christ is preached and its power is displayed in the changed lives of those who preach it, there is an irrefutable argument for it.

We are Christ's letter of recommendation. The medium of its writing is not with ink, but with the Holy Spirit. The place of the inscription is not on stone or paper, but on the heart. It is from thence that all our actions spring. If the heart is right, the whole man will be right. If, then, God has written His truth on our hearts, it will be reflected in the thoughts of our head, the deeds of our hands and the course of our feet. Our work, our words and our walk will conform to a new pattern of life.

Since we are Christ's letter, consider the purpose of a letter. Letters express our minds and in this sense we are to be a living expression of the mind of Christ.

In every letter, certain things are important.

The first is legibility. Every letter should be so plainly written as to prevent possibility of error in reading it. If it is blurred and scrawled in illegible characters, its purpose is defeated. Similarly, there should be about us a legibility of life. When our lives are filled with the scrawled deeds of inconsistent living, then our living has lost its purpose.

Then there is the attribute of sensibility. Every letter should be not only readable, but understandable. The thought and message it conveys must have a purpose. There must be a consistency of message or else it is of no use. The same is to be true of us. Our lives should present a plausible and sensible argument for Christ. In other words, our lives must make sense. They must express a common-sense definition of what Christianity is.

There is also the attribute of personality. A letter worthy of the name is the written expression of the writer. It reflects his personality. It reveals his soul. It takes what is inside and puts it into language which is an expression of his character.

In the letter of Christ which we are considering, it is Christ's Person which should be expressed through our personality. The message may not be written on engraved stationery and may not be dispatched in scented envelopes, but the medium is not the important thing. It is the message which counts. Nevertheless, we must not depreciate the importance of the best possible presentation of the message. We must keep before us the thought that as letters reveal personalities, even so our

lives are ''[epistles] known and read of all men'' and
should express the attraction and strength of the Person of Christ.

While the epistle of Christ refers to the collective
Church, we ought to remember that our individual lives
are to be so legible and so sensible in their transmission
of truth as to cause men to desire Christ.

At this point it can be said that Paul described rather
than defended himself and his ministry. One cannot sense
the slightest effort on Paul's part to engage in a selfish
debate over himself. He allowed his life to speak for itself. He unrolled his record and invited all who would,
friend and foe, to inspect it. He bared the innermost
recesses of his soul and invited them to examine his motives.

C. *The Divine Qualification* (verses 4-6)

1. Paul's Call (verse 4)

And such trust have we through Christ to God-ward.

Not only were the Corinthian converts a credential of
Paul's claims and career, but Christ was also. Paul was
fully accredited and he pointed out that the validity of
his ministry was substantiated by the Lord Jesus Christ.
This dated back to the Damascus road where he saw
Christ and was born anew. It was there he amended his
ways and from whence he went out to preach Christ. It
was this life-changing experience which gave Paul his
confidence. Any servant of Christ who has ever heard
the call of God in his soul will have a confidence that
nothing can shake. No matter how formidable the foe or
valiant the enemy, the call of God will hold him steady
and true.

2. Paul's Equipment (verse 5)

Not that we are sufficient of ourselves to think any thing as of
ourselves; but our sufficiency is of God.

The nature of Christianity is such that it requires an equipment beyond the ordinary. It is not a natural philosophy, but a supernatural life. From this fact Paul spoke of his own equipment as a preacher of such truth. He declared that he was not qualified to argue for it by his own natural abilities. This was in spite of the well-known fact that he was an honor student of the far-famed Gamaliel. Paul was no intellectual amateur. Neither was he a worldly novice. He knew life and was well trained, but all of this was not enough. He had to have more and so he said, "our sufficiency is of God." He claimed that all his qualifications were from God. A man who will make such a self-effacing claim is sincere and genuine.

Was Paul any different, in his position, from a modern minister of Christ? Of what should a minister's equipment consist? By all means, the best training he can secure. Yet, that is not enough. He may be well trained, but he is not well equipped until and unless he has had such a self-effacing and spirit-filled experience as Paul had. He, too, must say, "our sufficiency is of God."

The absence of this divine sufficiency undoubtedly accounts for much of our human insufficiency. Through God's sufficiency comes our efficiency. We may render a religious service without accomplishing a spiritual work. We may be humanly energetic without being divinely energized.

If we observe our natural life, we shall have a valuable lesson for our spiritual life. Broadly speaking, we are what we eat. We become like the environment about us. Man is literally from the dust of the earth, not only in his original creation, but from his daily food. "For this reason his physiological and mental activities are profoundly influenced by the geological constitution of the country where he lives, by the nature of the animals and plants on which he generally feeds'' (Dr. Alexis Carrel).

The same is true of our spiritual life. The new nature must have a new environment. It must have a new atmosphere and new food. It must have a new source of vitality if it is to function in its new activity. The new man in Christ cannot live on the same menu as the old man in Adam. The new service under the Great Commission of Christ cannot be rendered efficiently by the old efforts. The new service requires a new sufficiency. Paul says, ''our sufficiency is of God.'' He is saying in substance that you cannot run a church like you would a club. You cannot preach the Gospel like you would propound a philosophy. You cannot teach the Gospel like you would deliver a lecture. There is a spiritual technique peculiar to Christianity. Let us find it and then follow it.

3. Paul's Ministry (verse 6)

Who also hath made us able ministers of the new testament; not of the letter, but of the spirit: for the letter killeth, but the spirit giveth life.

When Paul said ''able ministers'' he was not egotistically referring to his own abilities. That would have been inconsistent with what has just been said. He was humbly referring to his competence as God's servant. Such competence as he had, he gratefully ascribed to God.

The significant thing about this statement is the phrase ''new testament.'' Paul was in reality a New Testament minister. That is as it should be. Obviously he was not an Old Testament priest, prophet or scribe. These offices belonged to another order, whereas Paul belonged to a new order. In this new order there was both a message and a new power with which to declare and proclaim that message.

The new sufficiency to which Paul had already re-

ferred is now described. It was "not of the letter, but
of the spirit." This tells us that the strength and power
of the ministers of the New Testament do not lie in the
letter of the law, but in the Spirit of God. In other
words, it is not the strength of a written code but the
energizing power of the divine Spirit.

There are few Bible verses more frequently abused
than the phrase "the letter killeth, but the spirit giveth
life." It is interpreted to mean the literal and the spiritual, or the actual and the allegorical. It is supposed
to say that we should not pay literal attention to the
text of the Scripture but should be governed by a spirit-
ualized meaning. Such is not meant at all. It is, instead, a contrast between Moses' law as a written code
of laws and the Gospel of Christ as energized by the
Holy Spirit. The "letter" is the law of the Old Testament. The "spirit" is the Holy Spirit of the New Testament.

In the light of this we observe that we have both a
new message and a new manner. The manner in which
the message is to be proclaimed is in the quickening and
energizing influence of the Holy Spirit. The personal
value of all this is its application to our daily Christian
lives. Whoever has Christ, has a new life and a new
power. However, having Christ does not necessarily
mean that Christ has us. We may be selfish Christians
instead of Christlike. We may be carnal instead of spiritual. We may be defeated instead of victorious. We
may be weak instead of strong. Our responsibility is to
make a complete surrender of ourselves to Christ so that
there may be complete consecration.

The Christian life proceeds from the Person of Christ.
Its inspiration is not in a code of written laws, but in the
companionship of a living person.

One of our modern philosophers propounds the idea
of religious behavior without a religious object. He

proposes that people lift their hearts in praise and worship without having anything or anyone definitely in mind toward whom those sentiments are directed. This would be an abortive worship. In fact, it would not be worship at all. It might be religious, but it would not be spiritual. Certainly it would not be satisfactory.

Man who was made in the image of God is restless until he rests in God. What is missing must be restored. The broken fellowship must be re-established. This is only possible through Jesus Christ.

No human personality is self-contained. It is not complete in itself. It must have Christ to be complete; consequently our intellect, conscience and affection are only complete in the Christ who has come to recreate us in God's image. The lost image is restored in Christ. Because "man shall not live by bread alone, but by every word of God" we have Christ as the Logos come to supply that need and satisfy our life.

The Christian conception of what the world calls a religious experience is something vital. It is a life and not a logic. It is an experience with God which is practically possible in every phase of life.

Someone has expressed it as the difference between a Christmas tree and a Christian tree. One has ornaments and the other has fruit. One is dead and the other is alive. One is attractive by artificial hangings and the other is fruitful through an inner life. There are a lot of religious Christmas trees hung with the ornamentations of artificial sentiments. Let us all be living and vital Christian trees, bearing the fruit, which is "love, joy, peace, longsuffering, gentleness, goodness, faith, meekness [and] temperance."

II. THE CHRISTIAN'S INSPIRATION (verses 7-11)

We have a threefold contrast between two ministries or administrations.

A. *Death and Spirit* (verses 7-8)

But if the ministration of death, written and engraven in stones, was glorious, so that the children of Israel could not stedfastly behold the face of Moses for the glory of his countenance; which glory was to be done away: how shall not the ministration of the spirit be rather glorious?

The administration of death was the law, while the administration of the spirit is grace. These two administrations are not concurrent, but consecutive; that is, they do not parallel each other, but one precedes and the other succeeds. They are neither identical nor interchangeable. They belong to entirely separate eras. They perform two distinct functions.

The law came by Moses—grace came by Jesus Christ. The law says: "Do, and live"—grace says: "Live, and do." The law says: "The wages of sin is death"—grace says: "The gift of God is eternal life." The law pronounces condemnation and death—grace proclaims justification and life. The law says: "Cursed is every one that continueth not in all things which are written in the book of the law to do them"—grace says: "Blessed [is the man] whose iniquities are forgiven, and whose sins are covered. Blessed is the man to whom the Lord will not impute sin." The law says: "Thou shalt love the Lord thy God with all thine heart, and with all thy soul, and with all thy might"—grace says: "Herein is love, not that we loved God, but that he loved us, and sent his Son to be the propitiation for our sins." The law addresses man as part of the old creation—grace makes a man a member of the new creation. The law deals with a nature prone to disobedience—grace creates a nature inclined to obedience. The law demands holiness—grace gives holiness.

The administration of the law which is identified with graven stone does not refer to the first giving of the law, but to the second. We forget that the law was given twice. When God first gave the law at Sinai, He wrote the law Himself on tables of stone that He had prepared, and He gave them to Moses amid accompaniments of thunder and burning fire and a mighty voice that filled the people's hearts with fear, so that even Moses himself said, "I exceedingly fear and quake." He called it God's "fiery law." It was absolutely rigid; its principle was: "Eye for eye, tooth for tooth... burning for burning, wound for wound." It was absolute intrinsic righteousness. Whatever a man actually deserved according to that law he was to receive. But before Moses came down from the mount, the people had broken the law. The first commandment was, "Thou shalt have no other gods before me. Thou shalt not make unto thee any graven image, or any likeness of any thing that is in heaven above, or that is in the earth beneath, or that is in the water under the earth. Thou shalt not bow down thyself to them, nor serve them" (Exodus 20:3-5), and before Moses reached the mount the people were dancing around a golden calf.

Moses knew if he had brought that law into camp, there could be nothing but condign judgment. That holy law would of necessity have demanded the death of the entire people, so Moses broke those tables on the side of the mount, and came down empty-handed. Then he became the intercessor for the people and pleaded with God to show mercy. The Lord said that He would destroy them but make of him a great nation. But Moses said, "Oh, no, if someone has to be destroyed, destroy me, and save the people," and in that he manifested the spirit of Christ.

Then he went up into the mount again for forty days, and this time God gave the law tempered with mercy. He gave it recognizing the fact that the people themselves would not keep it, but He provided with this second giving of the law a system of sacrifices whereby the penitent law-breaker could draw nigh to God with that which typified the coming into the world of His blessed Son.

It was still law, but it was law tempered by grace. It meant so much to Moses to find out that the Lord had thoughts of grace in His heart for the poor people, that when he came down from the mount his very face was beaming. He had learned to know God in a new way during those forty days. When the people saw the light shining from his face they were amazed; Moses put a veil over his face until he had finished speaking with them, and when he went before the Lord again he took it off. The apostle has told us why he did that.

There was a glory connected with this administration of law, but it was a fading glory. The glory that irradiated the face of Moses passed away. So then, if glory, even a diminishing glory, ushered in the administration of law, how much more can we expect the administration of grace to be glorious? Indeed, it is most glorious. It is haloed in a glory that will never diminish or disappear.

The Christian lives under the administration of grace by the Holy Spirit. Consequently, he has a permanent and abiding life. It is not subject to change or abrogation. It is the certainty of these things which is the inspiration of his life.

B. *Condemnation and Righteousness* (verses 9-10)

For if the ministration of condemnation be glory, much more doth the ministration of righteousness exceed in glory. For even that which was made glorious had no glory in this respect, by reason of the glory that excelleth.

This contrast reveals the effects of the respective administrations of law and grace. Law brings condemnation without salvation. Grace brings righteousness without retribution. The law revealed the justice of God. Grace reveals the mercy of God.

The law, however, was not the only instrument of this past administration. It had an altar as well. What the law condemned as sinful the altar atoned by sacrifice. The law brought the sentence of death. The altar brought the gift of life. Thus in the shadow of awful Sinai with its awesome thunderings and lightnings hides the love of God with mercy sufficient for any need. It was a foreshadowing of the Cross with its administration of grace.

C. *Past and Present* (verse 11)

For if that which is done away was glorious, much more that which remaineth is glorious.

One administration was by its very nature a passing one. It had a glory that faded. The other administration was by its nature permanent. The law rested its obedience in the old nature of man. Grace rests its conquest in the new nature of man.

Twice these immediate verses use the words "done away." What is done away? The law. It is not done away in the sense that its principles are not in force. It is done away in its relation to salvation. It is fulfilled in Christ and the Gospel. It is still unlawful to lie, murder, to be idolatrous and immoral. However, it is no longer required to keep the law in order to attain salvation. Whosoever is saved will respect the moral code which is contained in the law, but there is a new standard. It is Christ in us. It is the new life and not the old law.

The most thrilling aspect of the Christian life is the fact of its power of transformation. It is not a system of self-improvement. Instead, it is the inner power of a great transformation.

III. THE CHRISTIAN'S TRANSFORMATION (verses 12-18)

  A. *Transition* (verses 12-17)

    1. The Bold Speech (verse 12)

Seeing then that we have such hope, we use great plainness of speech.

Because of Paul's great hope in the Gospel, he was fearlessly outspoken. He was not reserved in his claims. He had a tremendous personal confidence because his faith had created a great hope. It ought to be so with every Christian. We need not wrap our feelings in ambiguous religious expressions. We can claim the fullest measure of blessing from our faith. We need not go about saying, "I hope I am a Christian," or, "I expect to be saved by and by." It is our right to use "great plainness of speech."

    2. The Fading Glory (verse 13)

And not as Moses, which put a veil over his face, that the children of Israel could not stedfastly look to the end of that which is abolished.

This refers to the time Moses received the law in the mount. In God's presence his face absorbed and reflected the glory of His person. When he returned to the people, they saw how his face reflected that presence, but the light it reflected was a fading and diminishing light. In order to prevent the people from seeing the fading glory, he put a veil over his face. When he returned to God's presence the veil was removed and his face again shone with a new radiance. The significance of this fading glory was seen in the transition of the law. It was only temporary. It was to pass away and in its place would come the Gospel which would reflect the face of Christ and through which its beholders would be transformed.

3.   The Veiled Face (verses 14-16)

But their minds were blinded: for until this day remaineth the same vail untaken away in the reading of the old testament; which vail is done away in Christ. But even unto this day, when Moses is read, the vail is upon their heart. Nevertheless when it shall turn to the Lord, the vail shall be taken away.

This refers to Israel as a people. They are, as a people, with a veil of obscurity over their minds. Wherever and whenever the Old Testament is read, its meaning is obscured because their spiritual senses are dulled.

This fact is one of the strangest anomalies of history. As a people the Jews are among the most brilliant in the world. They excel in art, science and literature. By a per capita count their skill and attainments exceed those of other races. They have distinguished themselves in all walks of life. In astronomy they have Sir William Herschel; in music Mendelssohn; in philosophy Maimonides; in statecraft Disraeli; in history Neander; in archaeology Cyrus Adler; in jurisprudence Baron Reading; in science Albert Einstein. These names are but a paltry tithe of those who could be summoned to prove the distinction of this remarkable nation.

When this national brilliance is brought to the Bible, which they have given us, there is a mysterious lack of understanding. The Old Testament is from their hand. The law and the prophets flowed through the mold of their mind, yet they cannot perceive their meaning. How strange! Apart from the explanation we have here of this phenomenon, the whole thing would be beyond our comprehension. Truly, their minds are blinded and there is a veil upon their hearts. The Jewish nation gave us both the Scriptures and the Saviour, yet their mind is dulled to the Scriptures and their heart is dead to the Saviour.

The veil, it is important to note, is not on the Scriptures but on the mind. It is universally impossible for these people to perceive the transitory character of the

Mosaic institutions. It is equally impossible for them to conceive the historical Christ of the New Testament as having any place in the Old Testament system. To them Jesus Christ is an impostor. Their Talmud teaches that Jesus was a wicked man, a sorcerer and an idolater. It further teaches that He is in hell and that His name should not be mentioned without saying, "May his name be blotted out and his memory." The New Testament is called "the margin of evil or a blank page of sin." But all of this is because of the veil which is upon their hearts.

How strange all this is! Israelites by the hundreds of thousands have read the Old Testament Scriptures. It is considered sacred and holy. The people have eulogized its patriarchs and memorialized its events. In doing this they have completely failed to see the delineation of their Messiah. Yet, Christ stands forth upon every page of the Old Testament. He is typified in its characters and symbolized in its sacrifices. He could say, "Lo, I come (in the volume of the book it is written of me,) to do thy will, O God" (Hebrews 10:7). He walked with two disciples, "And beginning at Moses and all the prophets, he expounded unto them in all the scriptures the things concerning himself" (Luke 24:27).

The ignorance and antagonism of the Jewish mind to this sacred figure has no natural explanation. It is not for want of evidence, nor can it be explained by lack of information. The ignorance is not mental but volitional. The problem is not intellectual but spiritual. Its solution is not in education but in regeneration.

The remedy is given in simple terms. "Nevertheless when it shall turn to the Lord, the vail shall be taken away." This refers of course, to the Jewish heart. Whosoever will take a deliberate step in faith to Jesus Christ will have the veil stripped away. The very Christ who is a stumbling stone to the Jews becomes the key of understanding. In Him the Scriptures become luminous and plain. Through Him a new life is received. By Him life takes on a new meaning.

Out of the Scriptures we gather such facts concerning Christ as should constitute an irresistible conviction in favor of Him.

He who made "all things" (John 1:3) in creation was "made flesh" to provide salvation (John 1:14).

He who made man was "made in the likeness of men" (Philippians 2:7).

He who made the law was "made under the law" (Galatians 4:4).

He who was "clothed with honour and majesty" (Psalm 104:1) was "wrapped in swaddling clothes" (Luke 2:12).

He who is the "Father of Eternity" (Isaiah 9:6, R. V., margin) became an "infant of days" (Isaiah 65:20).

He who came in weakness (Luke 2:7) will come in power (Revelation 19:15).

He who is "the wisdom of God" (I Corinthians 1:24) "increased in wisdom and stature" (Luke 2:52).

He of whom it is stated, "Behold your God" (Isaiah 40:9), was the subject of Pilate's statement, "Behold the man" (John 19:5).

He before whom "every knee should bow" (Philippians 2:10) bowed His knees, and washed His disciples' feet (John 13:5, 12).

He who "knew no sin" (II Corinthians 5:21), "did no sin" (I Peter 2:22), "was . . . without sin" (Hebrews 4:15), and "in him is no sin" (I John 3:5), "bare our sins in his own body on the tree" (I Peter 2:24).

He who was the earth-rejected One (John 19:5-6) is now the heaven-accepted One (Acts 3:21).

He who wore a "crown of thorns" (Matthew 27:29) is now "crowned with glory and honour" (Hebrews 2:9).

He who was "on the tree" (I Peter 2:24) is now on "the throne" (Hebrews 12:2).

He who "appeared to put away sin" (Hebrews 9:26) is "now to appear in the presence of God for us" (Hebrews 9:24).

He who came to "die" (Romans 5:6-8) will come to "reign" (II Timothy 2:12).

Everything in life depends upon the right point of view. Those who have stood at Inspiration Point in Yosemite National Park will concur that it is well named because it reveals and interprets the whole valley.

Astronomy was misconceived for thousands of years, because the earth was believed to be the center of the planetary and stellar universe. The moment the sun was seen to be the center of the solar system and the earth a planet moving around it, the confusion of the Ptolemaic gave way to the order of the Copernican. So, if in the pursuit of knowledge you take God as the center, the universe becomes a harmonious system. Atheism is a folly, intellectually as well as morally. The only rational interpretation of nature is to put God on her throne as Creator and Ruler.

In the intelligent attitude to personal life we must put Christ at the center. The Bible becomes life's inspiration point. Christ becomes the center of our spiritual system with all life revolving around Him in ordered sequence.

4. The New Liberty (verse 17)

Now the Lord is that Spirit: and where the Spirit of the Lord is, there is liberty.

When we have given Jesus Christ His rightful place, we find ourselves moving in a new liberty. The progress from Old to New Testament is a progress from law to liberty. Instead of regulation by an outer law, there is inspiration by an inner law. It is "the law of the Spirit of life in Christ Jesus.'' And as it declares here, ''where the Spirit of the Lord is, there is liberty.''

The outer law placed restrictions on outward conduct. It regulated conduct by a series of rules. The inner law of the Spirit transforms life within. It changes desires, affections and convictions.

This verse constitutes the Christian's emancipation proclamation from the bondage of the law. It declares our freedom. It liberates us from the law's precepts and penalties. It lifts us out of the sphere of legalism and into a new sphere where life is a free service of love.

This freedom is not to be misinterpreted as a license which permits the promiscuous and unbridled display of carnal desire. Rather, it is a liberty which inwardly causes us to desire and to do the very things the law requires. However, the motive and the motive power are different. The motive is love, not fear. The power is the Spirit, not the flesh. The Gospel not only gives us new motives but it puts within us a new motive power.

B. *Transformation* (verse 18)

But we all, with open face beholding as in a glass the glory of the Lord, are changed into the same image from glory to glory, even as by the Spirit of the Lord.

We pass from transition to transformation. The transition is general while the transformation is individual.

Let us examine the three steps in this transformation.

1. The Beholding—''We all, with open face beholding as in a glass the glory of the Lord.''

The ''we'' of the ''open face'' are none other than those who have believed and received Jesus Christ and are indwelt by the Holy Spirit. No others have this ''open face.'' All other faces are veiled. Only when we turn to the Lord is the veil taken away. He unveils us that we, like Moses, may behold the glory of the Lord.

The attitude of the open face is that of "beholding." This means to gaze. It is not glancing but gazing. It is not looking, but seeing. It is a steadfast gaze which takes time to absorb every detail.

That which we behold is glory in a glass. The glory we gaze upon is the glory of Christ. It is His perfect character. The place where the glory is seen is the Scriptures. In the previous reference to Israel, it spoke of their failure to see Christ when they read the Scriptures. Now, we of the unveiled face who read the same Scriptures, behold in them as one does in a mirror, the reflected glory of Jesus Christ.

Twice the Bible speaks of itself as a glass or a mirror. In James 1:23-25 it refers to the sinner and the mirror of the Word. Here it refers to the Christian and the mirror of the Word. When the sinner looks into the Bible, he sees his own image, sinful and vile. When the Christian looks into the Bible, he sees Christ's image. The sinner beholds and believes for salvation. The Christian beholds and surrenders for transformation.

One reason why many people do not read the Bible is because it exposes them. A mirror reflects what looks into it. How true it is we do not know, but we have been told that Queen Elizabeth for the last twenty years of her life refused to look into a mirror. The master of the royal mint had incurred her displeasure because his engravers had too faithfully reproduced her likeness, wrinkles and all, on a piece of money. The die was broken and, from that time on, no fragment of mirror was allowed in any room in the royal palace.

The Bible is a faithful witness to our sins. It reflects every defect and produces an inner conviction of personal deficiency. Because they are made uncomfortable by it many are afraid to see themselves as the Bible sees them.

    2. The Changing—"are changed into the same
       image from glory to glory."

The image which the Bible reveals to the people of the
unveiled face is the image of Christ. Gazing results in
changing. This change is not a superficial and artificial
facial reflection. It is transformation, not imitation.
It is an inherent change of character, not a mere reflection on our faces, such as Moses had. It is an inherent likeness, not a reflected one.

Our change is unto His likeness. This is a wonderful
thought. Think of a transformation that gives a character likeness to Christ. Beware of any cheap religious
imitation.

The change is gradual. It is from one degree of glory
to another. It is a continuous transformation. As we
momentarily behold, so shall we be momentarily
changed. It is not a sudden and instantaneous change
that comes in a flash.

There is a change which is instantaneous. It is the
change of salvation. That is the change of a moment,
but this is the change of sanctification and is a change
of degrees. The change which is salvation depends on
God. The change which is sanctification depends on us
in the sense that unless we keep a steadfast gaze and
maintain an unbroken fellowship we will not be changed.
There is another sense in which they both depend on
God, because salvation is God's work for us, while
sanctification is God's work in us. Let us never relax
our gaze, and we will never lack the charm of a character changed into Christ's image.

    3. The Transforming—"by the Spirit of the
       Lord."

This supports the previous contention that the change
is God's work in us. We are not changed by human
improvement. It is not the improvement of attainment

but rather the result of an inner change of character and is ''by'' the indwelling Holy Spirit.

It is our steadfast gaze into the Bible's mirror of revelation which brings the transformation of our character into the image of Christ. Let us be sure we do the gazing and God will be certain to do the changing.

If you desire a changed life, consider Jesus Christ. Fasten the gaze of your attention upon Him and you will become like that which you contemplate. The place of your gazing and contemplation must be the Bible, for that is where He is revealed.

4

THE LIFE THAT ENDURES SERVICE

2 Corinthians 4

Wherever you find running water, you find living water. When water becomes stagnant it breeds poison, sickness and unloveliness. The Christian who is active in service automatically falls heir to multiplied blessings that others cannot know. His life will be living, clean, sparkling and attractive.

What Christendom needs is a new emphasis on the positive side. It needs to perform rather than reform.

The service side of Christian experience is a normal phase of Christian life. Its place in II Corinthians completes a perfect triad. In Romans, salvation is set forth. In I Corinthians, sanctification is set forth. In II Corinthians, service is set forth. Salvation is God's work for us. Sanctification is God's work in us. Service is God's work through us.

We are not living a normal Christian experience until these three phases of God's work for and in and through the Christian are true of us.

The chapter holds four things before us.

    I. THE PERSONAL MOTIVE (verses 1-6)
    II. THE VICTORIOUS SERVICE (verses 7-11)
    III. THE INNER SECRET (verses 12-15)
    IV. THE ETERNAL REWARD (verses 17-18)

I. THE PERSONAL MOTIVE (verses 1-6)

Since this is a biographical account of a distinguished Christian, we shall find here not only the inner secrets of this man's soul, but also a cross-section display of motives and virtues for all Christians.

It seems so strange that a man of Paul's character should have been hounded by persecution from within the church. He probably suffered more from this source than from all the multiplied adversaries without. These experiences were more painful and more difficult to bear than anything he was called upon to suffer in the world. His motives were called into question. His character was vilified. His name was besmirched. His actions were reviewed with a critical scrutiny that had already prejudged and condemned him.

What Paul offered here in response to all this campaign of hatred and hindrance was not a defense, but a declaration. It was a declaration of motives. He reached into his soul and took out his innermost secrets for the inspection of all who cared for the truth. Many would not be impressed, for there are people who feed only on suspicion, envy and slander. They thrive on the troubles of others. They live to obstruct the processes of decency and honor. For these, all Paul could do was to state his ideals and leave the issue with God and then go on with his work, no matter what opposition or obstruction he met. It was a wise course and he is a wise man in this day who follows such a course. To cease one's constructive work to engage in debate and conflict with opponents is to play into the devil's hands.

We have before us:

A. *The Worker's Sincerity* (verses 1-2)

Paul was willing to let his record speak for his character. However, this is not always the final answer because there are many with brilliant records of visible results who have been prompted by the basest motives. Not Paul. He exposed his very soul. He was willing to reveal his whole heart. In doing so he spoke of two things.

1. Of Receiving the Gospel (verse 1)

Therefore seeing we have this ministry, as we have received mercy, we faint not.

Paul's motives were according to God's mercy. He had received great mercy at the hand of God. Once a proud Pharisee, boasting in the attributes of personal excellence and seeking to establish salvation by religious zeal, he had met the risen Saviour on the road to Damascus. That road for Paul was one of religious duty. He had been dispatched to put Christians in jail. On the road he had met Christ, face to face, and had become a changed man. He saw himself the chiefest of sinners and in his need turned to Christ and found what religion had previously failed to give him.

Paul had a very definite personal experience. It was not a theory gleaned from books. It was not an altruism learned from teachers. It was not a ceremonial developed by devotion. It was a life, a new life, a saving life received in the converting experience of the new birth.

Paul called attention to the fact that he received the Gospel, not only as a personal way of life, but also as a ministry. It came to him as something to pass on to others. He was resolved that the greatness of the mercy he had received would be the measure of the greatness of the service he would render. He was resolved that the man who ministered to others would be in keeping with the message he had received.

2. Of Living the Gospel (verse 2)

But have renounced the hidden things of dishonesty, not walking in craftiness, not handling the word of God deceitfully; but by manifestation of the truth commending ourselves to every man's conscience in the sight of God.

A false life is as bad as a false doctrine. To live the Gospel is just as important as to preach it.

The best recommendation of the Gospel is not how much we say about it, but how much it has done for us.

There is a good deal of heresy-hunting in our day. We do not deny the need of purity in truth, but an equal diligence is needed in holy living. The lack of holiness is just as deplorable as the presence of heresy. The Church needs a new orthodoxy—the orthodoxy of conduct which will match the orthodoxy of creed.

Paul received one thing and renounced another. He received truth and renounced evil. To have possessed the truth while practicing evil would have been a religious anomaly, therefore he renounced all underhanded dealings and unscrupulous practices. He did not tamper with God's message. He did not preach for personal gain. He had nothing personal to promote. He was out and out for God.

It was by such a life that Paul dared to vindicate his claims to apostleship. Whether or not all men were persuaded, did not matter. What mattered was that Paul was right. To be right matters more than to be thought right. If all the world thinks us wrong, it is still important to be right within ourselves. You can never hope to win the unqualified approval of all men, but you must be true to God and yourself.

Here is a lesson we must not fail to learn. Let us examine our souls and establish our standards. Let us be sure that we have become right with God and within ourselves. In such a fortress of personal purity and righteousness we can defy the world.

The problem of infidelity and agnosticism is more than an intellectual one. Consequently its solution is more than education. We have so secularized our religious approach to the world that it amounts to nothing more than mental improvement. Christianity is that and much more. It is spiritual before it is intellectual. Until we see this and get men spiritually right, all our other well-intentioned efforts will be in vain.

B. *The Unbeliever's Blindness* (verses 3-4)

Two identifications are made. Paul identified those who are blind and the one who causes the blindness.

1. The Blind (verse 3)

But if our gospel be hid, it is hid to them that are lost.

This declares that where there are those who still wear the veil of unbelief when confronted with the Gospel, such blindness is not the fault of the Gospel; neither is it necessarily the fault of the messenger of the Gospel. The fault lies with the hearer whose veil of unbelief identifies him as being unregenerate.

Unbelief and unregeneracy go together. Such unbelief as is mentioned here is not the question of mere doubting. It is bold and deliberate opposition. It reveals an incapacity to understand, which has been deliberately created by continuous unbelief.

You cannot educate people into Christianity any more than you can ceremonially induct them into it. It is a problem of character and nature, which in turn is a problem of spiritual genetics.

This is serious business. It speaks of men being lost. What does the Bible mean by being lost? Is it a state of personal vagueness that is cleared up automatically? Indeed not. It is a matter of eternal destiny. The word "lost" is the one you use when you speak of an article which has disappeared and gone out of your possession.

The Gospel makes another designation and calls other men "saved." These are they who were lost, but have since been recovered. The difference between being lost and being saved is the Gospel. Our attitude to it is the

most serious thing we have ever faced. Our acceptance
of it will be the most profitable choice we ever made.

2. The Blindness (verse 4)

In whom the god of this world hath blinded the minds of them
which believe not, lest the light of the glorious gospel of Christ, who
is the image of God, should shine unto them.

The blindness was not arbitrarily imposed by Satan.
It was self-chosen. They were willing subjects of satanic propaganda. It would be unthinkable that God
would permit men to exist in a state wherein they could
not believe and be saved. Wherever a state of personal
blindness exists, it is because men permit it to be so.

Satan is given a unique title—"the god of this world."
Literally, it means "the god of this age." He is not, of
course, the god of the universe. He is the self-chosen
god of this age. It is a law of the eternal ages that if
we do not make room for Jehovah-God we will have room
for the evil influence of Satan. If we reject the light we
will become victims of darkness.

Satan reigns today. He reigns in the hearts of men,
in fashions, in philosophy, in nations, in commerce, in
every enterprise and individual that does not accept
the truth. Because of this there are two contrary and
antagonistic forces in the world—those who are blinded
by the god of this world and those who are enlightened
by the Gospel of Christ.

Christ is declared to be the image of God. Christians
are the image of Christ. You may choose your character and your destiny. It is a matter of deliberate
decision. To be a Christian takes a decision. Decision
determines direction. Direction determines destiny.

C. *The Source of Light* (verses 5-6)

There are two sources of light.

1. The Divine Source (verse 5)

For we preach not ourselves, but Christ Jesus the Lord; and ourselves your servants for Jesus' sake.

Paul's declaration was plain. The substance of his message was Christ. Christ is the source of light for the lost. This fact defines the Gospel. It is not philosophy. It is not religious history. It is the very substance of the infinite. It is something which goes back of man to God. It is what we call the centrality of the Gospel. It centers in Jesus Christ. Christ is not a religious relic for veneration. He is the revolving point of all modern Christian experience. Without Him Christianity is but another religion.

2. The Human Source (verse 6)

For God, who commanded the light to shine out of darkness, hath shined in our hearts, to give the light of the knowledge of the glory of God in the face of Jesus Christ.

The Christian is the source of light, not as its originator, but as its beacon. We are beacons for the world's vast spiritual darkness.

The fact referred to here includes two great events. It includes creation and redemption. God commanded the light to shine out of darkness at the creation. The light which shined out in a creative way has now been made to shine in, in a redemptive way. The light of creation has become the light of salvation. The light placed in the heavens has become a light placed in our hearts. The light which was material has become moral. The physical light of the sun has become the spiritual light of the Son. The universal light has become the personal light.

Thus we have the God of creation and the God of redemption revealed to us as one. It means that having received physical life as a result of creation we receive spiritual life as a result of salvation. The first birth requires a second birth.

Here is a revelation of great importance. The Cross was planned as carefully as creation was planned. It is as necessary to our scheme of life as the sun is to the solar system. Your place in the material world is proof of your responsibility to the moral world. If God is your Creator, He must also be your Saviour. The argument is almost endless, but it addresses itself to the conscience of all men and women.

The medium by which this light of salvation is to reach the world is the Christian. The light that hath shined out and shined in, is in us that it may be given to others.

How necessary that the light shine in! Others cannot see it until we have it. We cannot reflect what we do not see. We cannot give what we do not have.

It is important to understand the nature of the light, as well as the source of it. It is described as "the light of the knowledge of the glory of God in the face of Jesus Christ." Previously Christ was spoken of as the image of God. Now He is spoken of as the light of God. The light was reflected in the face of Christ. What is reflected from His face is intended to be reflected from our faces to the world about us.

Our motives are the most important thing in our efforts. Achievement is robbed of its glory whenever it is prompted by an unworthy motive. Even failure may be a thing of glory, if we go down to defeat with our souls unsullied and our colors flying.

We should inspect the motives which prompt us in doing today's task lest we be found guilty of that which is unworthy of our high calling.

Whatever the motive, we must be prepared for adversity and opposition. One can be prompted by the highest and best ideals and yet find himself opposed by enemies who will impugn those motives and obstruct his efforts. This is inevitable. It will be found inside as well as outside the Church. If we are prepared for this kind of opposition, we will save ourselves the jolt of disillusionment later. Adversity lies athwart the advancement of every high-minded person. The best efforts you can put forth will be opposed by the worst efforts of both carnal and natural man.

If Jesus and Paul were the victims of such opposition, who are we that we should escape? It is in the very nature and pattern of events that we shall meet resistance.

The presence of these things is the promise of greater things. The very forces that oppose you will be the elements that advance you. The eagle sets its wings to take advantage of the wind and, by the wind that opposes him, he soars higher than before.

II. The Victorious Service (verses 7-11)

Here are two facts:

A. *The Vessel and the Treasure* (verse 7)

But we have this treasure in earthen vessels, that the excellency of the power may be of God, and not of us.

Paul likened himself and his fellow Gospel workers to fragile earthenware pots, unattractive in themselves, but valuable for what they contain. In Oriental countries, it was customary to keep gold and jewels in earthenware containers. They were ordinary clay pots used as vaults, but without intrinsic value. Their value was in the service they performed.

This was Paul's humble conception of himself. He did not wish to be thought of as someone important. He was anxious only to be a common container of a valuable treasure, the reason being "that the excellency of the power may be of God, and not of us."

The message is more important than the messenger. The treasure is more valuable than the vessel. The fortune is more important than the vault that holds it. The light is more important than the lamp that sheds it. The content is more important than the container.

In this case the vessel was Paul and the treasure was "the knowledge of the glory of God in the face of Jesus Christ." It was in Paul's power to give a disproportionate attention to the vessel which would have lessened the value of the treasure it contained.

While all this is indubitably true, we must not lose sight of the fact that the vessel has its importance. Paul was important to the early Church. Martin Luther was important to the Reformation. John Wesley was important to the world-wide revivals of his age. William Carey was important to the evangelization of India. Although they were only earthenware pots of fragile personality, they were indispensable to their times. So are you. You may be a very ordinary clay vessel. You may be crippled, or sick, or limited in many ways, yet you are indispensable in your place. There is a treasure for you to hold and to give. Be sure you hold it and be sure you give it. While you cannot emphasize the vessel over the treasure, you cannot overemphasize the importance of the vessel as a means of bearing the treasure.

The fragile character of the messengers of Christianity has always enhanced the divine character of the message of Christianity. In fact, one of the greatest proofs we have of the divine character of Christianity is the men used to establish it.

For instance, Jesus was not a blustering, bold conqueror who reduced His opponents to subservience by violence. He conquered by love. The apostles and disciples were not prominent or popular men. They were common clay vessels. They were enlisted from the ranks of ordinary men. Some were fishermen, others farmers or tradesmen. Only a few were men of distinction. It is written: "For ye see your calling, brethren, how that not many wise men after the flesh, not many mighty, not many noble, are called: but God hath chosen the foolish things of the world to confound the wise; and God hath chosen the weak things of the world to confound the things which are mighty; and base things of the world, and things which are despised, hath God chosen, yea, and things which are not, to bring to nought things that are: that no flesh should glory in his presence'' (I Corinthians 1:26-29).

The Bible was not written by the Egyptians or the Grecians or the Romans. Although the greatest library of antiquity was in Alexandria, and the most distinguished philosophers were from Athens, God passed by them and chose people from one of the lesser nations of the world to perform the greatest literary service of all time. Moreover, they were not a literary people, but a pastoral people without literary ambitions. They were men untaught in the learning of their day. Such was Hosea, the herdsman, and Peter, the fisherman. To choose such as these, God passed by the greatest minds of antiquity. He passed by Herodotus the historian, Socrates the philosopher, Hippocrates the father of medicine, Plato the philosopher, Aristotle the philosopher, Euclid the mathematician, Archimedes the father of mechanics, Hipparchus the astronomer, Cicero the orator and Vergil the poet. And why? Because they were not listening. They were such magnificent vessels that their efforts would be toward themselves. Hence we have peasants and common people whose fragile earthenware pots were chosen to hold the priceless truth of salvation.

Do not be surprised if the so-called intelligentsia are not following Christ today. There are many distinguished Christians, but it is still true that the roster contains ''not many wise men after the flesh, not many mighty, not many noble.''

By this fact there is opened to every one of lesser attainments a broad vista of opportunity. We have been

excusing ourselves because we lacked so much, when
the very things we lack may be our advantage. Moses
had to spend forty years in the desert unlearning the
forty years' training of Egypt. What you can do is not
necessarily measured by what you are in yourself, but
rather what you have in the way of treasure. The
earthenware pot which was Paul was only valuable because of the treasure it contained. It is so with you.

After all, there is a large place in life for common
things. The most vital substances of life are found in
common containers. In the old farm days, the vital food
supply of the family was stored in clay crocks. These
containers were not made of precious metal nor embellished with fine decorations. They were frail vessels
of clayware. Without them the life of the home could
not have been sustained. Thus the world can ill afford
to be without the common Christian who is a container
of God's message of salvation.

Let us reappraise our own importance as vessels of
clay which contain the priceless treasure of divine truth.

There is a natural reluctance in all of us to face the
inevitable fact that difficulty and adversity are a necessary part of life. Until we learn this fact we will be
constantly out of adjustment to the realistic facts of
life.

This is borne out in the next section.

B. *The Victim and the Victory* (verses 8-11)

We are troubled on every side, yet not distressed; we are perplexed, but not in despair; persecuted, but not forsaken; cast down,
but not destroyed; always bearing about in the body the dying of
the Lord Jesus, that the life also of Jesus might be made manifest
in our body. For we which live are alway delivered unto death for
Jesus' sake, that the life also of Jesus might be made manifest in
our mortal flesh.

It may seem strange to consider these noble men as
victims, but they were victims only to the point of the
nature of their experience. Out of their experience

their stature was greatly increased and their usefulness was enhanced beyond thought. Their faculties and abilities were sharpened and quickened by the grinding stones of adversity. The process was unpleasant, but the product was justifiable.

Ease is never a part of attainment. Comfort is never found in conquest. Discipline belongs to discipleship. In the process of our sanctification strength comes from our trials and victory through our adversities.

Paul described his experiences in such terms as to leave with us the thought that although he was a victim of adversity, he was also a victor in that adversity.

He was troubled, yet not distressed.

Although his foes pressed in upon him from every side, he was not hemmed in. With all the activities of his adversaries, he was not straightened in his own activities. It is the picture of a wrestler trying to crush his adversary. Paul was never vanquished by any of his adversaries.

He was perplexed, but not in despair.

Paul's circumstances often brought him to his wit's end so that he hardly knew which way to go or what to do, but never to the place of ultimate despair.

It is not unnatural to doubt, but it is not necessary to despair. It is possible to be bewildered and confused, but not necessary to give up hope and surrender the fight.

The margin rendering says: "not altogether without help or means." When you feel the weakest and effort seems futile and the cause lost, then remember you have at your command means to extricate yourself from your perplexity.

He was persecuted, but not forsaken.

Persecution and tribulation are inevitable experiences of life. Jesus said they would come. He further said that when they came, He too would come to stand with

us. Man's persecution means God's presence; thus
our adversity brings a new advantage.

He was cast down, but not destroyed.

This means to be struck down and beaten to the earth,
yet never eliminated or driven from the field of conflict.

By these things we can see how sorely the Christian
may suffer and how the multiplicity of adversity may
beset him, yet he is still victor.

Here, too, is the truth that victory is not what we
experience, but how we experience it. Triumph is not
escape from adversity, but it is bearing it to personal
conquest.

Paul found such words in the vocabulary of his experience as trouble, perplexity and persecution, but out
of these came victory and triumph.

This was not all. Paul further described his experience
as "always bearing about in the body the dying of the
Lord Jesus."

This was not a process of self-salvation, but the experience of sanctification. It was fulfilling what Jesus
had said must be true of His disciples. "If any man
will come after me, let him deny himself, and take up his
cross, and follow me" (Matthew 16:24).

The Cross is more than a pious sentiment. It is to be
a personal experience. The sphere of this experience is
not to be in our imaginations and pious reflections. It
is to be in our bodies. Paul said he bore these things
in his body. That means he felt the crucifying effects
of Christ's Cross in his feelings, appetites, activities and
desires.

This is practical piety. There is little to be desired in
a thumb-rolling piety that sits in the sanctuary and
never ventures life in the practical problems of everyday experience.

The purpose of experiencing Christ's death in our
body is to reveal Christ's life in our body. When we

die, He lives. These are not just pretty sayings; they are the laws of the spiritual life. Jesus said, ''Except a corn of wheat fall into the ground and die, it abideth alone: but if it die, it bringeth forth much fruit.'' The seed must die if it expects to live. We, too, must die to all our selfish ambitions if we expect the abundant fruitfulness of a noble life. No one can retain his own selfish ambitions and at the same time be inspired by the noble purposes of Jesus Christ. If He is to live through us, we must die in Him.

I am sure it has often been true of all of us, that we have passed through experiences we could not understand. We can understand only in proportion to our place in the will of God. Paul understood the purpose of his experiences very plainly. He said, ''For we which live are alway delivered unto death for Jesus' sake, that the life also of Jesus might be made manifest in our mortal flesh.'' It was God's purpose to display through Paul the excellencies of Christ's life. The immediate object of this display was the people of Corinth. All of Paul's pains and perils were to be the means of exhibiting to these Corinthians the life of Christ.

Here was life at its highest level. It was not life at its easiest, to be sure. The easy way is not necessarily the best way. After all, what does it matter that we have lived unless, in living, we have touched other lives for their good. Christianity is not a means of altruistic social service. It is the means of reproducing Jesus Christ in other lives. It may include giving bread and clothes, but it must not fail to reach the inner man while it is ministering to the outer man. Unless we do that, our social service is in vain, for the fundamental problems are of the character and not of the body. If we are careful to display the life of Christ in a crucified manner, it will be inevitable that we will also extend the mercies of Christ.

A great intellect linked to a low purpose will cause great havoc. Some of the greatest destroyers in the world have been men of great intellect. Their motives were low and consequently their percentage of evil was high. Harness a little intellect to God's purpose and God's will and it will outshine and outdo the most brilliant intelligence in the world.

Many people despair of doing any good because they lack education, polish and attainment. They despair unnecessarily. If they will take what they are and have, and link that to God's high purposes of the Christian life, they will be able to produce more and do more than the so-called intellectual giants of this world.

If you will align your littleness to God's bigness and your faith to God's power and your mind to God's Word, you will become a great power for righteousness and good. Oh, that we might have a generation of big little people! We have put altogether too much emphasis on the apparent bigness of men. We need to see the real proportions of strength and power that are possible to every common Christian.

III. The Inner Secret (verses 12-16)

Behind every great and profitably productive life lies a secret. Great lives are not the result of little accidents. They do not just happen. They are caused and the cause is discoverable and possible of emulation.

None will deny the impressive stature of a man like Paul. There are intimations in his writings of physical unimpressiveness. His person was not very striking. Be this as it may, there is an undeniable greatness about him that inspires every sincere soul.

There are at least five elements in the secret of Paul's stature.

A. *The Secret of Self-Crucifixion* (verse 12)

So then death worketh in us, but life in you.

Paul was conscious of having a continuous experience of crucifixion. It was not flesh crucifixion, but self-crucifixion.

This is the beginning of all success. The secret of success is the capacity to lose one's self in the service of something greater. This is true because power always dies through devotion to self. To merely annihilate one's self is not enough. Hindu fakirs do this. All religions teach self-annihilation. Only Christianity promises resurrection. When we die to ourselves, Christ lives in us. We exchange our mediocrity for His might and power.

Someone asked George Mueller for the secret of his life. He replied with these significant words: "There came a time in my life when George Mueller died, utterly died. He died to all his selfish plans and ambitions. When he died, Christ lived through him. This is my secret."

B. *The Secret of Intense Faith* (verse 13)

We having the same spirit of faith, according as it is written, I believed, and therefore have I spoken; we also believe, and therefore speak.

Here is an important item—it is believing what we say. To speak is not enough. The magic of words comes only from the might of faith. Paul believed and therefore he spoke. He was utterly sincere. His were not empty platitudes and meaningless phrases. His utterances were supported by the earnest conviction of his heart.

C. *The Secret of a Glorious Hope* (verse 14)

Knowing that he which raised up the Lord Jesus shall raise up us also by Jesus, and shall present us with you.

Paul was inspired by the glorious hope of the resurrection. It accounted not a little for the tremendous power of his life. He saw beyond this life into another. He did not think of death as something which frustrated one's labor of life. Death for the Christian merely transferred life and labor into a better and more productive sphere. It gave an inspired incentive to activity and service.

D. *The Secret of Self-Forgetfulness* (verse 15)

For all things are for your sakes, that the abundant grace might through the thanksgiving of many redound to the glory of God.

Paul considered his sufferings as being beneficial and helpful to others. When he suffered, others were helped. Thus he could say, "All things are for your sakes."

One has reached an advanced state of grace and experience when he can consider his misfortunes in the light of advantage for those whom he serves.

This conviction sustained Paul in many a difficulty. He was glad to have misfortune if his experience could profit another.

We live in a world where the philosophy of survival for personal interests is at the fore. Nations fight for great slogans, yet the purpose is self-survival. The law of the jungle is the law of civilization. We have espoused the principles of the beast. There is collective bargaining and collective security, but a lack of personal integrity to guarantee the bargain and the security.

Paul lived the larger life with the interests of others at heart. This is an indispensable item of real success.

E. *The Secret of Spiritual Strength* (verse 16)

For which cause we faint not; but though our outward man perish, yet the inward man is renewed day by day.

Facing tremendous difficulties and working under the terrific pressure of life, Paul said, "We faint not."

He never flinched. He never lost heart. He did not swerve from his purpose. This is perfect perseverance. It is the secret of perfect poise.

Paul gives us the contrast between the outer man and the inner man. The onslaught of opposition wears down our natural physical life, but the inner life of the spirit is growing stronger under the pressure. Destruction and construction are simultaneous. While the outer is being destroyed, the inner is being renewed. It is being renewed by prayer, by the promises of the Word of God and the presence of the Spirit of God.

It is a great comfort to know that while eyesight grows dim, hands become unsteady, limbs weak and memory faulty, the inner man of the soul grows stronger through a day by day renewal of spiritual strength.

It is possible under the strain of normal life, with its problems and its pressure, to be constantly renewed and strengthened in the fortress of the soul. So long as we maintain clear channels of communication between ourselves and God, the struggles may batter us, but they cannot defeat us. We may suffer every disadvantage of adversity and be victorious through it all.

The measure of this victory is the measure of a day by day contact with God. Religion by the year, the month and the week is an impossibility. Christianity is something by the day. To really know what Christ can do, let it be a day by day walk with Him.

We must be careful to keep things in proportion. Christians are easily persuaded to throw their vision out of perspective. Too many of us adopt the philosophy of escapism. We try to escape the reality of today by dwelling in the glories of tomorrow. These glories and the ultimate triumph are certain to come, but we must live and face today.

In Pasadena a man faced the police court on a fail-ure-to-provide charge. It was brought out in the testimony that he was a member of a religious sect which predicts the end of the world in the very immediate future. For that reason he believed it unnecessary to provide for, or to educate, his nine-year-old son. What a tragic misconception such an attitude is! The inevitable consequences of the future are neither reason nor excuse for us to shirk the responsibilities of the present. We are to live and work today. The intelligent hope which the Bible gives of tomorrow should be the incentive and inspiration for today.

The world is full of fearful men and women who go through life under dread and strain. The Christian is full of hope. His hope is based upon knowledge, conviction, experience and faith. He is confident and resolute. He knows today's afflictions are not the final experiences. Tomorrow will dawn with its glory, therefore he goes through life unafraid. With this sort of faith, he not only walks on, but works on.

IV. THE ETERNAL REWARD (verses 17-18)

Two situations are contrasted.

A. *The Affliction and the Reward* (verse 17)

For our light affliction, which is but for a moment, worketh for us a far more exceeding and eternal weight of glory.

The affliction is light while the glory is an eternal weight. The affliction is momentary while the glory is eternal.

Three important facts are contained in this verse.

1. The Present Experience—"our light affliction, which is but for a moment."

The present experience is but a "light affliction" and in duration is "but for a moment." All of this is relative. Our momentary experience is not minimized. The Bible admits affliction. It is placed in the vocabulary of Christian experience. We are not to think it away, nor say that it does not exist. Facts are facts to faith. Our experience is but a light affliction in relation to the "far more exceeding and eternal weight of glory." Affliction is an intolerable, unbearable and hopeless experience apart from the "far more exceeding and eternal weight of glory." It is an endless experience of agony apart from the eternity of glory that succeeds it.

This means that the present moment is to be an experience of glorified affliction. Paul referred to actual experiences. He used such words as trouble, perplexity, persecution, being cast down and experiencing self-crucifixion. These may come to us in many forms. For one they may be body pains and for another mental suffering, but it is all affliction "for a moment."

2. The Unseen Condition—"worketh for us."

The word "affliction" is translatable into our English word meaning "pressure." Affliction is a pressure that works for us and not against us. Usually we consider affliction an adversity, but in this view it is an advantage. It is sometimes difficult to see this at the time of the affliction and during the pain of it, but it is a fact as true as the Bible itself.

3. The Future Prospect—"a far more exceeding and eternal weight of glory."

The future prospect is beyond all proportion to the present experience. If the experience is affliction, the prospect is glory. Suppose we began to look at our experience in the light of this far view. Measured by its pain, it is unbearable. Measured by its glory, it is a privilege.

Here is a new philosophy of pain. It glorifies the drabness and the dinginess of life.

B. *The Temporal and the Eternal* (verse 18)

While we look not at the things which are seen, but at the things which are not seen: for the things which are seen are temporal; but the things which are not seen are eternal.

This verse explains and amplifies the secret of this philosophy of pain. It is while we are looking at things that are not seen that we can understand the meaning of our affliction. If you fasten your hopes on the seen, there is scant hope for you. Life has no meaning. Pain is a bandit of the soul—a bandit that robs you of pleasure.

This new explanation of life is only possible when we understand that "the things which are seen are temporal; but the things which are not seen are eternal."

There is something exceedingly sensible about this. It is the reverse of the usual idea about life. Materialism bases its hopes upon what is tangible to the five senses, yet everything you touch will crumble and everything you see will pass away. Only that which faith sees and the heart holds, will be eternal.

The Christian bases his hopes on the unseen. This and this alone will last. It will endure when all else fades and fails. Money, time and talent invested in the unseen will remain. It is beyond the chemical dissolution of material things.

Of course, this does not mean to suggest that for the rest of our natural lives we should sit down and stare off into space. We are still in a world of practical reality. While we handle the seen, we do it in the spirit of the unseen. While we build houses, mend clothes and keep books, we do it with the devotion of the unseen. Thus we transfer the material into the spiritual and the seen into the unseen and the temporal into the eternal.

Glorify pain and magnify labor in the light of these facts and life will hold a different meaning.

5

THE LIFE THAT ENDURES DYING

2 Corinthians 5

Intelligent and successful Christian service rendered to thè world for God is not blind devotion to duty. It is not the regimentation of our resources at the expense of our reason. Instead, it is a way of life which holds a comprehensive view of the future as well as the present. It is the possession of all our faculties and the surrender of them to God. It is the use of what we have by the indwelling power of the Holy Spirit.

Throughout all the experiences of adversity which came to Paul, he had the knowledge that those things would not always be as they were. He saw a time coming when life would take on a different form. By faith, he could glimpse the future. As he saw that future with its new status for those who had died, it had a profound effect on the present. It gave him new incentive and inspiration for the life to be lived now.

In this chapter both death and life are spread before us.

    I. THE INTERMEDIATE STATE OF THE DEAD (verses 1-10)

    II. THE INTERMEDIATE NEED OF THE LIVING (verses 11-21)

I. THE INTERMEDIATE STATE OF THE DEAD (verses 1-10)

Our consideration is directed to five provisions of this state.

A. *A New Body* (verse 1)

For we know that if our earthly house of this tabernacle were dissolved, we have a building of God, an house not made with hands, eternal in the heavens.

There is to be what is properly termed an intermediate state of life between the Christian's earth-life and his heaven-life. It is that phase of his existence which immediately follows death on earth and precedes life in heaven. That is to say, it is a life in heaven, but not the final life in heaven.

By intermediate, we mean something in between. When death occurs to the Christian, it separates him from the temporal, although it does not immediately unite him with the eternal. The immediate effect of death is to release the person from the body. That person is then immediately brought into the presence of Christ. It says in verse 8, "to be absent from the body, and to be present with the Lord." This presence with the Lord is not a bodily presence, because that will not occur until the resurrection. In other words, we do not receive our new bodies until the dead shall be raised incorruptible.

Between the time the body is buried and the time it is resurrected, the Christian is in this intermediate state. Where he is, is described only by such words as we find here, "to be absent from the body, and to be present with the Lord."

The Bible is not being rightly interpreted when it is claimed to teach either a purgatory of purification or an oblivion of unconsciousness. We do not cease to be. Our bodies are not we. The body and the person are as building and occupant. Bodies die and are buried and pass through dissolution. The occupant moves out.

Paul is giving us a contrast between our old and our new habitations. He is telling us the difference between our body of dissolution and our body of glory. He calls our body a tabernacle.   This tent-body is the one in which we are making our pilgrimage from earth to heaven. Some day it will be taken down and laid away and covered up. At that time it is to be dissolved, or loosed. It will be loosed from its present form and shape and will return to the elements from whence it sprang at the creation. In its place we will have, not a tent, but a building. The tent was temporary. The building will be eternal. The tent was left on earth. The building will inhabit the heavens. The tent passes through disintegration which reduces it to its original chemical state of common soil. The building possesses the qualities of Christ's resurrection which are incorruptibility and immortality.

Of necessity, there must be an interval of time between our departure from our dissolving earth-body and our inhabitance of our eternal heaven-body. During this interval we are in conscious existence, although we are not yet in our resurrection bodies. We are not floating around in space as invisible spirits without the capacity of speech or action. Neither are we asleep or unconscious in a temporary lethargic state. We are to be very much alive and very near to Christ, for to be "absent from the body" means to be "present with the Lord."

To simplify the matter we can put it this way: While death disembodies us, it does not immediately embody us with this "house not made with hands." This "house not made with hands" is not another temporary body, for the reason that it is called "eternal." It is our final habitation, but it will not come to realization until the rapture and the resurrection.

B. *A New Desire* (verses 2-4)

For in this we groan, earnestly desiring to be clothed upon with our house which is from heaven: if so be that being clothed we shall not be found naked. For we that are in this tabernacle do groan, being burdened: not for that we would be unclothed, but clothed upon, that mortality might be swallowed up of life.

The new desire is not the desire for death which dissolves or unclothes the spirit. That would be unnatural. The Christian is looking beyond death for the time when he will be clothed with his new body. Death as a natural process, is not the hope of the Christian, for death disembodies and disrobes. It is the resurrection and the rapture which the new desire longs for, because the resurrection and the rapture will bring us this building which is "an house not made with hands."

Death is not the hope of life. Death is a curse. It answers no questions and settles no problems. However, for the Christian, there is a hope that came through the death and resurrection of Christ, his Saviour. It is this hope that sustains him. It is what the resurrection will accomplish that he yearns for. It is the ultimate answer for all the aspirations of faith.

No one can take an indifferent attitude to what the Bible says of our origin and our destiny, and expect in that indifferentism to have an intelligent and practical view of life.

We cannot escape the connection between origin and destiny. We cannot be wrong about one and right about the other. If we mistrust the Bible's declaration about origin, how can we believe what it says about destiny? In the Bible, both are linked together. Origin is contained in a process of creation, while destiny is contained in a process of redemption. The Creator is revealed as the Redeemer.

The materialism of our age would persuade us to believe in an origin of force. The logical end of that kind of a creation is to begin as a beast and to die as a beast; to come out of oblivion and to go out into oblivion; to come up from the soil and to go back to the soil.

The Bible speaks differently. While man's body came

up from the soil, because God made it from dust, his soul, or his personality, came down from God. He was made in God's image and likeness. His creation was after a divine pattern. Having lost the image of that pattern it produced the necessity of redemption. Redemption is man's re-creation after a divine pattern. Having been created in the image of God, man is redeemed and regenerated in the image of God's Son.

The spiritual part of that new image comes through regeneration, while the physical part of that new image comes through resurrection.

C. *A New Assurance* (verse 5)

Now he that hath wrought us for the selfsame thing is God, who also hath given unto us the earnest of the Spirit.

The Christian's assurance of a time when mortality will be swallowed up of life is not postdated. It is, in fact, predated. He has the assurance of that hope now. It is something in which he lives. He lives for it and he lives by it. It is not something away off in a mystic future, but something within.

The resurrection is the consummation of regeneration. It is the final phase of God's plan of redemption. We were redeemed with all of this in mind and the God who is working out this redemption in us at the present moment has not left us without a very definite assurance. He has, in fact, given us a guarantee that we will be brought to the consummation of His plan.

The guarantee is "the earnest of the Spirit." This earnest is two things in one.

1. This Earnest Is a Pledge

The word "earnest" means "surety" or "pledge." A surety is security which one gives for the performance of a promise. It is making one's self legally liable for the performance of a contract. In other words, it is a pledge to consummate what one has commenced.

In Bible times when a man bought a piece of land he would be given a handful of its soil as the assurance of its ultimate possession. In turn he would deposit a consideration of money as the assurance of its ultimate payment.

The earnest money of any transaction or agreement was a part payment of the whole sum promised. It became the pledge to the receiver by the giver that the contract or promise would be carried out in due time. According to Blackstone, the prepayment of a mere penny would legally bind a contract.

2. This Pledge Is a Person

It is the Holy Spirit who has been given to us as the pledge.

As a rule, the pledge given and received was the same in kind as the ultimate payment. In this case, the ultimate contract which God made with us was life and the pledge which He has given that He will fulfill that contract is the life of the Holy Spirit.

A pledge is always a preview and a foretaste of what is to come. In this case, we can expect to have the presence of a heavenly life on earth.

The Christian is not to pursue his discipleship because he expects to get to heaven. The end of the Christian life is not merely life hereafter. It is life here. It is not a means to an end. It is the end itself. It is something for this world, as well as for the next.

The proof and pledge of this intention is the presence of the Holy Spirit in everyone who is a child of God.

Here is the ultimate purpose of the Holy Spirit. He is God presently with us. He is God powerfully with us. He is God reverently with us. Let us not prostitute this sacred relationship by fanatical orgies of hysteria and hypocrisies. Let us not treat the Holy Spirit as some phenomenon of emotion which we can reproduce in a state of ecstasy. The Holy Spirit is God come to His temple. He is God as the present guarantee of our coming consummation. He is God who comes to us the moment we come to Him. He is God as the indwelling presence of every Christian at the moment of the new birth. As such an indweller at such a moment of birth, He is the foretaste of what we shall have and what we shall be at the resurrection.

Because of this fact, Christian experience is not something that merely gives us the expectancy of eternal life. It is eternal life. It is that right now. It is so because every pledge is the same in kind as the ultimate payment. It is a foretaste of the coming life. Therefore, what we are to be is what we have now. What God is going to do for us He is doing in us. The physical transformation of the resurrection has its anticipation in the spiritual transformation of regeneration. We who are to be changed into His likeness are now being changed "into the same image from glory to glory, even as by the Spirit of the Lord."

In this way the Spirit who is the present pledge of the future resurrection of the Christian, is also the present power of the daily transformation of the Christian.

If you will remember that the Holy Spirit is a pledge and not a promise, you will never find yourself in any spiritual difficulty concerning which many err. He is not a promise to be expected. He is a pledge already given. He was promised and in fulfillment of that promise He was given. The promise thus became a gift and the gift a fact. The fact is something to be enjoyed. We do not seek Him but we should yield to Him. We cannot rightfully seek what has already been given, but we should yield and surrender all our faculties and members to His transforming power.

When we do this we will experience that transformation of character which is the anticipation of the transformation of body that will occur at the resurrection.

In this light, the pattern of Christian experience becomes very plain and beautiful. It becomes a complete and glorious picture. It balances the present with the future. It gives the present an equality with the future. It puts experience and expectation on the same level. It dignifies the Christian life to the degree of nobility.

We have been told that the only thing of assurance is the present. The future has been described as vague and fluctuating uncertainty. It is all of this to the natural mind, but not to the Christian. Christianity is a philosophy of faith which reduces the future to the present. It is not so to sight, of course, but it is so to faith. It is not something which is going to happen. It has already happened. It has happened in a personal and individual sense.

Notice how confidently Paul spoke of death and what follows. In the first verse he used the words, "for we know," while in the sixth verse he used the words, "we are always confident." It is the knowledge and confidence which Paul had. He did not have all the facts of the experience before him, but he had the faith of a spiritual experience in him. Until the facts materialize, faith is sufficient. Faith is "the highest act of reason."

D. *A New Sphere* (verses 6-8)

Therefore we are always confident, knowing that, whilst we are at home in the body, we are absent from the Lord: (for we walk by faith, not by sight:) we are confident, I say, and willing rather to be absent from the body, and to be present with the Lord.

Notice the force of these opening words: "Therefore we are always confident." Why this continuous confidence? How did it come? What gave Paul this complacency and contentment in the face of certain death? Was he basing his confidence on his personal morality, or on his life's labors? Not at all. He was

102 *Second Corinthians: Where Life Endures*

confident because of God's work and his witness. God's
work was the redemption of Christ. Paul's witness was
the inner witness of the Holy Spirit, for he had the
"earnest of the Spirit."

The present phase of Christian experience is the tene-
ment phase. It is the body phase. When Paul spoke
of being "at home in the body" he made an important
distinction between himself and his body. His body was
not Paul any more than your house is you. Paul was
a spiritual personality who lived in a physical body
just as you live in your house. The body is the vehicle
of the soul—the vehicle which makes it possible for the
person to act, speak and live a normal earth-life.

Some day we shall have no more use for the body.
We shall be disengaged from it. We shall go on while
it goes back to the soil out of which it came.

Until we go on, and while we are here awaiting that
summons which will cause us to vacate the body, we
walk by faith. Sight is the common way. Faith is the
uncommon way. Sight is the way of flesh. Faith is the
way of the Spirit. Sight is the world's way. Faith is
the Word's way. Whatever is common to sight is uncommon to faith. Sight relates to the temporal, faith
to the eternal. Sight relates to the seen, faith to the
unseen. Besides this, faith not only sees the unseen, it
also sees the seen. It is a spiritual sense for two worlds.
If you walk by faith, you can walk in two worlds at once,
whereas if you walk only by sight, you walk in one world.

Faith is not only a way to life, it is a walk through life.
Whosoever walks by faith has the most comprehensive
and practical way of life. He is not an impractical religious visionary, but one who has linked hands with
God.

To walk by faith does not mean to walk in blindness.
It means to walk with another sense of sight. It is not

walking in the dark, but walking in the light. It is exchanging eyesight for Godsight.

From these immediate Scriptures which speak of the believer's presence with Christ at death, we gather these comforting details about this intermediate state.

1. It Is an Immediate State

It occurs immediately after death. To be immediately absent from the body is to be immediately present with Christ. There is no long or short interval of punishment or unconsciousness in between.

2. It Is a Personal State

Death releases the person from the body and he goes on into Christ's presence as a complete personality.

3. It Is a Conscious State

Presence means consciousness. To be in the presence of Christ means to be conscious of Christ's presence. There would be no point in saying that we go into His presence unless we go consciously.

4. It Is a Preferred State

Paul spoke of being "willing rather" to be absent from the body in order that he might be present with the Lord. He said that he preferred death to life. In fact, he said to the Philippians that he had "a desire to depart, and to be with Christ; which is far better" (Philippians 1:23).

The fact that we can be present with Jesus Christ proves that He must exist somewhere in body and in person. This proves the further fact that when He died He must have been raised. Thus, all of these things tie together. There is a continuity of truth that we cannot escape. Our personal hope is bound up in the historical fact of the resurrection.

The Christian faith in its purest and truest terms

asserts and proves the resurrection of Christ as the basis for all our subsequent hopes. If He does not live, we cannot live. If He does not have a resurrected body, we cannot have a resurrected body.

Something must put a great compulsion upon us or we will become ordinary people whose lives and labors will matter little in the world.

In the next verses of this chapter we are approaching the compulsion of the Christian which is found in the fact of our impending death.

The urgency of this recalls to mind an advertisement which appeared in a national weekly magazine. It bore the picture of a beautiful farm with its well-built barns, its fields, cattle and fowl. To one side stood the farmer and his wife contentedly surveying a tornado shelter. It was well-built, strong and substantial with its door open and inviting its builder to seek its protection at an instant's notice.

Underneath the picture were these timely words: "Tornado shelters are built when the wind is not blowing."

It is so in the best of lives. Those who live conspicuously do not wait until death is approaching to get ready to meet God. They do not wait until the doddering days of old age to employ themselves in the Master's service. Death is an appropriate incentive for life, but you cannot wait until you are about to die. It is anticipated death which incites activity.

E. *A New Incentive* (verses 9-10)

Wherefore we labour, that, whether present or absent, we may be accepted of him. For we must all appear before the judgment seat of Christ; that every one may receive the things done in his body, according to that he hath done, whether it be good or bad.

Paul had an incentive which prompted and inspired him in his labor. In fact, it went behind his labor to his ambitions, because the word translated "labor" is the word for "ambition." His ambitions were prompted and energized by a great thought. Whether it was life or death, prosperity or adversity, health or sickness, he labored to be well pleasing to God.

This is revealed in the words "accepted of him." Paul, like every other Christian, was already accepted in Him, but now he expressed himself as being ambitious to be accepted of Him. The first acceptance was the result of God's work for us; the second acceptance will be the result of our work for God. One acceptance indicates our standing, the other indicates our state. The one was God's responsibility, the other is our responsibility.

It is impossible to go through life selfishly and recklessly, giving no consideration to God, and then expect to have His approval. Consider how many are doing this very thing. They throw God a kind religious thought one day out of seven and consider themselves religious, yet they live lives of reckless abandon. It is a fool's philosophy. No one who has ever seriously considered his life in the light of this teaching would flaunt its sacred standards. Instead, God's pleasure would become his pleasure; God's will, his will and God's way, his way. Furthermore, whosoever makes these things the measure of life will find the fullest measure of pleasure, contentment, peace and usefulness.

Paul believed in the future and he determined to let the future have a practical bearing on his life. He realized that somewhere his life and deeds would be reviewed and he ordered his life accordingly. If we really believe as Paul believed, we too will live with the same thing in view. What a vastly different world this would be if every Christian began to order his life, from this day on, with that in mind. The reason for this purpose is expressed in verse 10: "For we must all appear before the judgment seat of Christ."

At this point we must be clear in understanding that the judgment spoken of now is the judgment of Christians and not sinners. The judgment of sinners will take place at the Great White Throne (Revelation 20:11). We must also clearly understand that here the Christian will not be judged for sin in respect to salvation. That took place on the Cross. Here, it is a judgment in the form of a review or adjustment. It is a judicial judgment for the purpose of making such adjustments as were not made before. Here the believer must face unconfessed sin. Here he must adjust all the differences with fellow Christians which were not settled in the flesh. Here he must be brought into a perfect relationship with God as a prelude to the life of the eternal ages. Here any uncompleted work of sanctification must be finished. Here too, he must "receive the things done in his body." These are things done by means of the body. The body with its five senses is the vehicle of the soul, and whatever has been done through this medium will be reviewed in the light of the standards of the Gospel. If our deeds have been of the character of gold, silver and precious stones, we shall receive a reward. If, on the other hand, they have been of the character of wood, hay and stubble, we shall "suffer loss." However, the loss suffered is not the loss of our salvation, but the loss of our reward.

The Judgment Seat of Christ is an expression which had a local significance to these early Christians. It referred to the tribunals of the Roman magistrates— tribunals which were august representations of justice.

It was, first of all, a place. The technical word used here is "bema" which was a tribunal. The "bema" was a lofty seat on an elevated platform usually at the end of the judgment hall, so that the figure of the judge could be seen towering above the crowded room.

It is also a process. As a result of our appearance

before this "bema," we shall be seen in our true light. We shall be stripped of all disguise and pretense. All the trappings and gaudy coverings of religious hypocrisy will have been dissolved and we shall be seen as we are. There will be no further pretense or sham. The last great assize will reveal us in the blaze of reality.

This place and process has a time. It will be when Christ comes. We do not go immediately from death to judgment, nor to our reward. There is an interval of time between.

Let it be clearly understood that this process is not to discover whether we are Christians, but rather to reveal the true character of our Christianity. The judgment is not held to determine whether our characters are good or bad, but whether the deeds done in the body are good or bad. Even this does not mean good or bad in the sense of worthiness or worthlessness. In this manner life's labor will be reviewed to discriminate and separate those parts of our lives which have been lived for eternity or for time. Only the eternal will survive. Only the labor and the deeds of common occurrence about the home and shop which have been done in consecrated surrender will have the quality of survival.

All this is very solemn. It is something that should give us no carefree ease until we are determined to live today according to the pattern of this judgment.

There will be a judgment. Every act leaves its mark upon our souls. In the natural world there are ample evidences of this. "Every part of the material universe contains a permanent record of every change that has taken place therein, and there is no limit to the power of minds like ours to read and interpret the record. A shadow never falls upon a wall without leaving thereon a permanent trace, a trace which might be made visible by resorting to proper processes."

If this is true in our material world, consider how much more likely it is true in our moral world.

Having presented the future and its consequences of life, Paul next reviewed the present and its responsibilities of life.

If the foregoing matters of death and judgment are true, we must do something about them. In the following verses Paul has told us we must do something about these matters right now. Thus we have the compelling motive of evangelism, personal and public.

After all, death should not be considered as some isolated part of life, or as something appended to the end of an earth-existence, or even as some sort of an executioner. In the Christian scheme of things, death should be considered as belonging to life. It is that which ushers us from one phase of life to another. It is also that which shuts off opportunities that will never come again. Death therefore gives a new imperative and incentive to life. We must live right if we expect to die right.

II. The Immediate Need of the Living (verses 11-21)

Here we have two points to be considered.

A. *The New Motive in Winning Men* (verses 11-15)

It is a threefold motive.

    1. Sincerity (verses 11-12)

Knowing therefore the terror of the Lord, we persuade men; but we are made manifest unto God; and I trust also are made manifest in your consciences. For we commend not ourselves again unto you, but give you occasion to glory on our behalf, that ye may have somewhat to answer them which glory in appearance, and not in heart.

Paul began from a rather awful premise. He said, "Knowing therefore the terror of the Lord, we persuade men." He referred to his own fear of the Lord. It was the knowledge of the coming inspection of motives and service at the Judgment Seat of Christ which drove him into tireless labors.

It was not blind fear, such as one has of a tyrant. It was that intelligent view of the final ending and final inspection and final sifting that would come. Paul understood God not as some vacillating deity who could be moved back and forth between wrath and love by man's prayers. Paul knew Him as a God of love and justice with His justice grounded in His love. He was a God who demanded sincerity, honesty and integrity in His people. Paul knew it. While Paul knew it was possible to live a deceitful life of service here, deluding the people and serving for gain, he knew it was impossible to deceive God. He knew the "terror of the Lord." That is to say, he had both a holy and a wholesome respect for God's opinion of his life and he purposed to adjust his life to that opinion.

Is there anything to fear in God? At this point personal opinion is worthless. Let God speak. The Bible says, "The fear of the Lord is the beginning of wisdom." It further says, "It is a fearful thing to fall into the hands of the living God." Does it mean that God is a dread tyrant? Not at all. It is one side of the question only. Through your house flows an invisible current of power. It lights your lamps, heats your toaster and powers your washer. That is one side of this current. If, under adverse circumstances, you were to take hold of the naked wire through which that invisible current flows, it would cause death. That is the other side of this current. Knowing God is life. Not knowing God is death. Yes, there is something to fear in God.

There is something for the Christian to fear. He should fear the consequences of a misspent life. He should fear the inspection of the judgment if his life and service are insincere and hypocritical.

From this wholesome and holy fear of God, Paul

moved to win men. He said, "We persuade men." It was, literally, "to win men." Henceforth every thought, word and act of his life were to be part of a campaign of persuasion. At all costs he would win men from the slavery of sin and the kingdom of Satan.

So far, the motive was personal. It was because Paul wanted no blood on his skirts that he sought to persuade men. It was because of the answer he must make at the judgment that he wanted his life to be free from blame.

But there was more to Paul's motive in winning men than this.

2. Unselfishness (verse 13)

For whether we be beside ourselves, it is to God: or whether we be sober, it is for your cause.

Paul would win men for the Lord's sake and also for their own sake. As he looked across the vast expanse of paganism and noted its cruelty and crudity he was moved to action by the thought of what these pagans could become. We imagine that he saw men as Jesus did; he saw them not as they were, but as they might become. Jesus never hesitated to undertake the regeneration of any man. No one was too low, too vile, too hopeless or too helpless for Him.

Out in the Black Hills of Dakota the distinguished sculptor, Gutzon Borglum, supervised one of the most stupendous memorials on earth. The greatest thing Borglum has ever done, however, is his head of Lincoln in the capitol at Washington. He cut it from a block of marble which had long been in his studio.

It is said that into that studio came an old Negro woman to dust. She had been accustomed to seeing that marble block standing there and for days had not noticed it. One morning she came in and saw to her astonishment and terror, the unmistakable lineaments of Lincoln appearing in the stone. She ran to the sculptor's secretary and said, "Am dat Abraham Lincoln?" "Yes," said the secretary, "that is Abraham Lincoln." "Well," said the old woman, "how in de world did Massa Borglum know dat Abraham Lincoln was in dat block of stone?"

The sculptor saw in that block of stone the possibilities of a face, just as Jesus saw in the men of Galilee the possibilities of mighty men and women once they were touched by the Spirit of God.

3. Love (verses 14-15)

For the love of Christ constraineth us; because we thus judge, that if one died for all, then were all dead: and that he died for all, that they which live should not henceforth live unto themselves, but unto him which died for them, and rose again.

Literally, the first clause means "the love of Christ overmasters us." That is to say, it makes us helpless to do otherwise than to win men. When we are overmastered by Christ, it means that His life is ours, His love is ours, His truth is ours, His will is ours and His passionate concern for men is ours.

It does not mean that Paul had some kind of an insipid religious love for Christ. It speaks instead of Christ's love for the great lost and dying world overwhelming, overcoming and overmastering this man until he is driven by a master passion. Paul became consumed to the very core with an idea. He became gripped by an unshakable conviction.

What is this conviction? Paul stated it in these words, "If one died for all, then were all dead." Christ was this "one" and the people of Paul's day and ours were and are these "all."

Christ died because they were dead. They were spiritually dead. Through death Christ made it possible to release His life so that these who were and are dead might live. The means would be faith and the medium would be men like Paul and men and women like you and me.

There needs to come to each of us a new sense of conviction and a new force of compulsion. Love needs to overmaster us. The world's need must overwhelm and appall us. We must be driven or we shall be dried up in the selfishness of our own souls.

B. *The New View of Life Which Comes to Those Won* (verses 16-21)

There is a new view of life when one becomes a Christian. One does not stay in the same place. One does not live the same way. One does not have the same ideas. With a new nature there come new activities. It would be impossible to conceive of the Christian life continuing on the same basis as the old life. There is a new person indwelling us. There is a new pattern for the old ways. There is also a new power for the old weakness.

It is of this new standard of life that we now speak.

1. A New Creation (verses 16-17)

Wherefore henceforth know we no man after the flesh: yea, though we have known Christ after the flesh, yet now henceforth know we him no more. Therefore if any man be in Christ, he is a new creature: old things are passed away; behold, all things are become new.

The new life gives a new way of measuring men. It says in effect, in verse 16, that henceforth we appraise no man by human standards.

Some people use this text in a ridiculous way. They say, "Henceforth know we no man after the flesh," as though it meant that we ought to regard our brethren with contempt. Nothing of the kind is meant.

Prior to becoming Christians some of the men Paul knew were involved in ignoble living. They lived according to the standards of the flesh. Now they were

Christians. A change had come. The old judgments and measurements were therefore out of date. This is also true when a man becomes a Christian today. The old standards of judgment and the old distinctions are gone; the old liabilities and the old inclinations are gone. From now on we measure a man by a new standard, not by the flesh, but by the Spirit; not by social birth, but by the new birth; not by his advantages, but by his activities; not by himself, but by Christ. In Christ we judge a man, not by what he has, but by what he does; not by what he was, but by what he is.

Why is all this so? How do we get this measurement? It comes because of a new manhood. The new manhood is described in these thrilling words, "Therefore if any man be in Christ, he is a new creature: old things are passed away; behold, all things are become new."

Here are two great and important facts about a Christian.

a. He Is a New Creation

This is definitely settled in the words "If any man be in Christ, he is a new creature."

Here is a fact far removed from a narrow religious concept. The word "creature" is interchangeable here with the word "creation." Either or both are correct. We have then a new creation as against the old creation. The fountainhead of life of the old creation was Adam. From him sprang the physical race down to our present day, but it was a race of sinners. It was a race of living dead men. They lived physically but were dead spiritually. The need was for a brand new creation. It called for the introduction of a new kind of life. That kind of life came in and through Jesus Christ. Now we have, according to the law of spiritual genetics, a new creation of which Christ is the fountainhead. It is a race of new people. They are people with a new nature.

b. He Lives in a New State of Life

This is definitely settled in the words "Old things are passed away; behold, all things are become new."

Thus a profound and radical change has begun in the personality of the believer. The new birth has implanted a new life. This new life has displaced the "old things" of the former life such as habits, appetites, desires, ideals, inclinations, etc. This new life, furthermore, has brought in an entirely new set of appetites, desires, ideals, inclinations, etc. If the believer will nourish this new life of the Spirit which has come by the new birth, these new appetites, desires, ideals and inclinations will grow and develop and become the controlling factor of life. What is true of the believer will be true in the believer.

This is the crucial point of Christian experience. Someone will say that when he became a Christian he did not immediately get rid of a bad temper or a quick tongue. The new birth does not annihilate the old nature, but brings in a new nature to control it. Henceforth the old tempers and the old tongues have a new master and are under a new control. Their passing away is both a crisis and a process. The crisis of their passing away comes at the new birth when the new nature is implanted to displace these faults from their old seats of control.

Potential control and conquest lie within us the moment we are born again. However, actual control and conquest depend on the degree to which we will yield ourselves to the transforming power of our new nature. This is a daily process and experience. We still have to contend with old things while we live in the new things, but control and conquest is the result of the indwelling new nature of Christ.

Do not think for a moment that the statement, "Old things are passed away," means that there is no more evil in you or in the world about you. Were this true it would belie the consistent teaching of the Bible as well as the facts of life. The truth is that a new kind of life in Christ has come and it has within it the power and blessing of new things.

It is a new relationship with God. He becomes our Father instead of Creator. It is a new rule of action, a new object in life, a new experience of pleasure, a new thrill of living and a new satisfaction of heart. This and a multitude of other new things come in the wake of this new life.

This new life gives us a new set of ideals. Now they are Christian ideals. "Ideals are like stars; you will not succeed in touching them with your hands, but, like the seafaring men on the desert of waters, you choose them as your guides, and following them, reach your destiny." We too, must keep these new ideals before us.

It is very important to be clear on one point. This new creation begins with Christ. The Bible says, "If any man be in Christ, he is . . ." What he is depends on where he is. His new manhood is the result of a new relationship. His new existence and experience do not begin with a new resolution to be good or with a new course of studies in religion. They begin in Christ.

It is important to know that of all God's creatures man is the only one who has the capacity to understand Him. Man was made in God's image and for God's presence. Man possessed an affinity of life by which there was instant and perfect understanding. He did not have to try to decipher a message from the stars, nor labor in agonizing prayer, nor make long and holy

pilgrimages to some sacred spot. Man was not divine
but the presence, the light and the knowledge of God
were in his soul. Because of these, we read in the early
chapters of Genesis of God's communications to Adam
and of Adam's conversation with God.

The curtain is drawn on that picture and following
it is man hiding in fear and finally fleeing from that
trysting place under condemnation. Instead of communication it is condemnation.

Now we have another picture. Since communication
has been broken by condemnation, we are presented
with the possibility of reconciliation. The hiding and
fleeing man is invited to stop beside a Cross, and be
reconciled. With reconciliation will come the communication of a new life, a new relationship and a new experience with God.

There can be no communication with God on the
creature-basis. That basis has short-circuited the lines
of the soul. But when one comes to God on the child-
basis, having been born again, he is in instant contact
with the infinite.

You can get clearance for your soul at a place called
Calvary. It is of this that these immediate verses
speak.

2. A New Ministry (verse 18)

And all things are of God, who hath reconciled us to himself by
Jesus Christ, and hath given to us the ministry of reconciliation.

The simple meaning of this statement may be put
into six words: He reconciled us to reconcile others.
This is every Christian's ministry. It belongs to all and
not to some. It is the simple plan that underlies the
whole scheme of world evangelization. Our reconciliation should lead to others being reconciled.

There is a dignity of deity about this that lifts it
above ordinary religious service. It is a cause that

proceeds from Christ and was not invented by a church committee.

The word "ministry" has a very significant meaning. It really means "charter." Charters are certain rights granted and guaranteed by the sovereign power of the state. It may be a charter to carry on a certain kind of business or a benevolent organization. In any case, it specifies the purpose of the business and then states certain lines and limitations under which this business is to be carried on.

In this same sense the Christian Church and the Christian have been chartered to conduct the King's business. The charter of the Church is the New Testament. The business under this charter is here described, in part, as "the ministry of reconciliation."

The need for reconciliation begins in the fundamental wrong of life. That wrong is sin. Reconciliation presupposes separation and separation presupposes an obstruction. There is a separation between God and man. This is not a religious myth. The New Testament says, "The carnal mind is enmity against God: for it is not subject to the law of God, neither indeed can be." This "neither indeed can be" means that there is a spiritual obstruction between God and man. Until that obstruction is removed there can be no reconciliation. Until there has been a reconciliation there can be no communication. We cannot enjoy God. We have no basis for a real prayer life. We have no place of satisfaction.

The thing to do then is to get rid of this obstruction between man and God. In the first place, what is it? For one thing, it is not ignorance. You do not have to be made wise. The obstruction is sin. It is not only a defect in your nature, it is an obstruction. It is an obstruction between man and God, between man and his fellow man, between man and himself.

The fact of this obstruction goes back to verse 14 where it says, "Because we thus judge, that if one died for all, then were all dead." The dead need life and the process of giving that life is by incarnation and regeneration. By incarnation Christ partook of our nature. Through His passion as one of us He brought reconciliation. Then by regeneration we partake of His nature. Thus, by His sharing our life we are able to share His life.

3. A New Message (verse 19)

To wit, that God was in Christ, reconciling the world unto himself, not imputing their trespasses unto them; and hath committed unto us the word of reconciliation.

The message of reconciliation which we possess and are to pass on to others is the disclosure of a wonderful thing. It is not a message about a lot of rules to follow. It does not speak of a long list of penances. It is not full of abstract religious sayings. It is not centered about some mystical idea of God. It is the simple and understandable fact that "God was in Christ, reconciling the world unto himself."

This means incarnation. None of us can completely comprehend God as a Spirit, but all of us can be happy about God as a Man. Thus it came to be when Christ came, for "God was in Christ." This puts salvation on human terms.

On God's side there was incarnation in order that there might be reconciliation. But what about man's side? He had nothing to do with providing the means of reconciliation, but he must provide something which is necessary for the operation of reconciliation. That one thing is faith and includes repentance and trust. It is a willingness to leave the old life and a readiness to take the new life.

The immediate result of this reconciliation is twofold. One is described here in the words, "not imputing their trespasses unto them." This means the canceling of the record of transgressions of which all men are guilty.

God not only cancels the record of evil, He also commences a new record of good. He puts to our credit by imputation the righteousness of Jesus Christ. This is our new capital of character on which we may draw for the needs of our life.

This is not all, for a righteousness imputed, without a righteous nature imparted, would be abortive and futile Christianity. We are not only given Christ's righteousness, but His nature.

This high view of Christian experience should lead each of us to an earnest review of his life. There can be no place in such a life for willful and known sin. After all, Christianity is more than a creed. It is conduct. To be in Christ means to be out of sin. To be reconciled to God means to be settled in a new life and separated from an old life.

When Lord Halifax came to the United States as Great Britain's ambassador, Americans understood the significance of an ambassador possibly as never before. With a great conflict raging to determine the course of national destinies, this man was chosen to represent his country in its crisis. His mission was to smooth our relations so as to secure the most aid with all possible speed.

Lord Halifax's presence meant almost as much as his words. As a matter of fact, he did not make a public utterance until months after his arrival. He symbolized something. He stood for something. All of this had its unconscious effect upon us.

What Lord Halifax was in a political sense, Christians are in a spiritual sense. It is this idea which is exploited in the following verses.

4. A New Title (verse 20)

Now then we are ambassadors for Christ, as though God did beseech you by us: we pray you in Christ's stead, be ye reconciled
to God.

We are envoys for Christ. An envoy is one who
speaks for another. In this case, we are to speak for
God. God is appealing to the world, through us, to be
reconciled. The message which we bear is "Be ye reconciled to God." We are saying this in Christ's place and as
His representative. If this is so, then it ought to be done
as we think He would do it. Jesus would not insult
people, or abuse them, or make Himself ridiculous and
His message a farce by fanatical outbursts. He would
speak today as He did in His day. He spoke with simple
and unstudied dignity. He spoke sincerely and straight-
forwardly, fearlessly and without favor.

Someone who had spent a long time seeking a church
for a satisfying message remarked, "Successful churches
are those whose clergymen set forth uncompromising
Christianity, sticking closest to Christ's difficult but
challenging teaching. That is the asset of the church.
The more vigorously a church proclaims it, the more
people respect and follow that church."

Jesus had a passion for men. His passion was that
men might be reconciled to God. No doubt, Jesus was
interested in men being well housed, well clothed and
well fed. He was interested in all the social needs of
mankind. However, we also know Jesus did not spend
His time directly on these things. He concentrated on
the spiritual, for when the spiritual condition was
right the social aspect would be right.

There are three attitudes we may take to life. One
is rebellion. We can rebel against existing conditions
and revolt against God and man in atheistic hatred.
This makes anarchists and communists. It leads to
destruction and chaos. It is both false and wrong.

Another attitude is resignation. Like the ancient Buddhists and Stoics we can say it must be so and there is nothing we can do about it. This makes slaves out of human beings and the kind of pawns that dictators use in their game of power politics.

The other attitude is the Christian way of reconciliation. This is the basis of the transformation which takes place in lives touched by Christ. Paul, as Saul of Tarsus, was a religious anarchist, set to destroy the new Christian sect, but he was brought to see that he was not fighting men. He was fighting God Almighty. He became reconciled and in that reconciliation was marvelously transformed into a mighty force for good. His case has since been duplicated times out of mind. Here is the hope of the world.

5. A New Condition (verse 21)

For he hath made him to be sin for us, who knew no sin; that we might be made the righteousness of God in him.

This is difficult to understand, but wonderful to consider. It tells of our new condition as the result of our new creation.

a. Christ's Sinlessness—"who knew no sin."

Sinless is what He was by character and life. Not once was a black mark chalked against Him. He never needed to confess a sin and never needed to take back a misspoken word.

b. Christ's Sinfulness—"he hath made him to be sin for us."

Here is a wonderful thing. In some mysterious manner Christ became identified with world-sin. He bore both its guilt and its penalty.

Where did this identification with sin take place? It was at His crucifixion.

At His incarnation, Christ through His virgin birth,

escaped being what we were. Through His unnatural birth He did not have our natural life. All men are born sinners but Christ was born sinless through His virgin birth. Only through this can we explain His sinless life.

At His crucifixion, Christ by His death, voluntarily became what we were. It was here that He, a sinless man, became identified with our sinfulness. That identification was retroactive because it affected all who had come before. It was also prospective, because it affects all who come after.

It is important to keep clear that the focal points are the incarnation and the crucifixion. They are the cradle and the Cross. One takes in the fact of the virgin birth which is the only possible explanation of Christ's sinless life. The other takes in the fact of His remarkable death. He did not die either of violence by the Roman crucifixion or of natural causes through disease. He died of His own deliberate will. We read in Luke 23:46, ''Jesus . . . said, Father, into thy hands I commend my spirit: and having said thus, he gave up the ghost [or breath of life].'' This giving up of life was the accomplishment of the atonement. It was the one supreme offering of a sinless life to meet a world's obligation to sin.

> c. Our Righteousness—''that we might be made the righteousness of God in him.''

This is the result. Because He was made our sinfulness, we are made His righteousness. How much of our sinfulness was He made? All of it, the very depravity of it. How much of His righteousness are we made? All of it, the very divinity of it. It is all or nothing. Jesus' crucifixion was not a dress rehearsal. He was sin and not merely sinful. He was the very hell of sin. It was more than a cloaking of Christ with the garments of our guilt. It was His becoming what we were. Apart from this we cannot understand Him crying, ''My God, my God, why hast thou forsaken me?''

Likewise, the effect is more than the cloaking of the believer in an artificial righteousness. It is our birth into a character righteousness. As He became what we are, so we become what He is and are said to partake of the divine nature.

This is indeed most wonderful. We may not be able to comprehend it but we thank God we can apprehend it. We may not be able to understand it, but thank God, we can believe it.

6

THE LIFE THAT ENDURES LIVING

2 Corinthians 6

Employment is a major concern. We need employment for economic reasons and to this end we prepare and extend ourselves. There is another kind of employment which should give us a restless concern. It is the employment of our lives in the service of life. None escapes this category of service. We may be business managers or housewives engaged in the most preoccupying duties. Still, there is the question, how are we investing life?

First of all, let us simplify it. We should not complicate it by thinking in terms of specialized service. The best use of life should be our urgent concern. Right now, it is a question of its best use in the present channel and the present place. It is the best use of the housewife's life, the lawyer's life or the clerk's life.

The beautiful thing about it is that we can begin right where we are. We can begin by making the Bible live through our life. It is very common to eulogize the Bible. There is something better than praising it and that is permitting its message to get into our soul and come out in our life. There is something better than defending the Bible; it is becoming living transcripts of its transforming power. The most practical point of contact between the Bible and this tragic world is the point of its practical demonstration.

This chapter falls into three equal divisions.

I. LIFE'S RELATIONSHIP (verses 1-2)
II. LIFE'S EXPERIENCES (verses 3-10)
III. LIFE'S ASSOCIATIONS (verses 11-18)

I. LIFE'S RELATIONSHIP (verses 1-2)

There needs to be restored to each of us the sense of obligation and the dignity of work. This does not pertain to secular work alone, but to the spiritual as well. To a large degree we have ceased being workers, to become religious drones.

What tragic words were in that requiem which Marshal Petain pronounced over fallen France: "Our spirit of enjoyment was stronger than our spirit of sacrifice. We wanted to have more than we wanted to give. We tried to spare effort and met disaster." The cause of Christ languishes in a wounded world for lack of valiant workers who might, if they would, bring such a flood of truth as would sweep out the evil forces of this moment. We prefer enjoyment to sacrifice. We would rather have than give.

Notice here two things which Paul was and which we might become.

A. *The Place* (verse 1a)

We then, as workers together with him.

Paul was God's fellow worker. This is the noblest employment of life. It is a life-linked labor with God. Paul was not a wandering religious star without place or purpose. He was not running his own religious show. He was a "worker together" with God in the channel of service which was the accepted order of that day.

We, like Paul, should not merely be working for God, but with God. This indicates a place of great honor. There are many who can say they work for Henry Ford but only a few who can say they work with him. To realize this is to recognize the exalted place of Christian service.

To be a worker with God requires concentration and co-operation. Consecration recognizes the worker's need of power and preparation. Co-operation recognizes the character of the work to be done.

The work to be done has just been described in the closing verses of the previous chapter as reconciliation. As such, it is primarily a spiritual work to be done with individuals. It is not at first a social work to be done with the masses. Reconciliation is an ambassadorial mission to men as individuals. It is this phase of our work which we must keep clear and pure. We must never allow ourselves to be employed in anything less than this.

B. *The Plea* (verses 1b-2)

. . . beseech you also that ye receive not the grace of God in vain. (For he saith, I have heard thee in a time accepted, and in the day of salvation have I succoured thee: behold, now is the accepted time; behold, now is the day of salvation.)

When Paul besought these people that they "receive not the grace of God in vain" he suggested a peril possible to a great many professing Christian people. This remark, remember, was addressed to the Corinthians and not to pagans, and it concerned their failure to enter into all the advantages of grace. Grace provided reconciliation and with it a life of fruitful employment with God. One might receive this grace in vain by accepting it without appropriating it or by failing to live so as to show he was a new creature with old things passed away and with all things new.

The remark that follows, part of which is quoted from Isaiah, is quite generally misapplied. A correct exegesis requires us to remember that Paul was speaking to Christians. He was reminding them, and us, that this whole age is both the "accepted time" and the "day of salvation." Whoever is not concerned with his work as ambassador, is receiving the grace of God in vain. Such a one is failing in his mission. He is misusing his life.

God has here and now provided reconciliation through Christ. This reconciliation is waiting for ambassadors to carry it far and wide. It is waiting for acceptance by those who need to be reconciled.

The other aspect of this verse is equally allowable. If this is the day of reconciliation's offer, it is also the day of its acceptance. If "the day" is an age of grace, then it is equally true that the age has its days.

Man lives a total of 25,000 days, more or less. Of all these days there is a great day of decision that marks the shape of destiny. That day is now. Grace is offered now. Christ is available now.

At this point we are given a description of experiences which came to one man in the course of his life and labors. These experiences run the gamut of pleasure to pain. They enroll a broad expanse of circumstances that follow one's fidelity to duty. They summarize the total feelings of a man who is all-out for God.

It takes courage to read this recital and say at its end, "God helping me, I too, will live so that my life will be the best credential Christ has in the world."

II. Life's Experiences (verses 3-10)

Paul has pleaded for a proclamation of the message. He has also shown the urgency of its telling and its hearing. There is yet another matter about which to be concerned. He who tells it must be careful of his own personal behavior, lest he hinder those who hear.

Paul set the theme of his own life in these words, "Giving no offense in any thing, that the ministry be not blamed: but in all things approving ourselves as the ministers of God" (verses 3-4b). If there were those who heard but would not heed the message to be reconciled to God, it would not be because Paul put stumblingblocks in their way.   No sin in his life would give a rejecter an excuse for rejecting the message. No scoffer would find comfort in the fact that Paul failed to measure up to his message.   After David's great sin Nathan said to him, "Because by this deed thou hast given great occasion to the enemies of the Lord to blaspheme."   Paul determined that this should never be said of him.

No matter how pure Paul's purpose and how noble his motives, he found himself the object of vicious plots, false accusations and diabolical designs.

It seems the more one determines to be true, the easier it is to become wrong, for life is beset by various obstacles that would seek to deflect one from his straight course.

The objective, remember, is for the messenger to furnish the best possible persuasion to believe.   It is true that the Bible has intrinsic power beyond that of any other message.   It is the power of life.   It is also true that the best recommendation of the power in the Word is the power of that Word in our own lives.

Paul set out to fulfill this noble purpose of giving no offense and in all things to commend himself as God's fellow worker.   Let us see what kind of experiences he encountered.   We may be surprised and shocked and not a little disturbed, but let us be daring to the end.

There follow three sets of experiences with nine particulars in each set.   These sets divide themselves as follows (Dr. H. A. Ironside) :

A. *Nine Testings of the Worker* (verses 4-5)
B. *Nine Characteristics of the Worker* (verses 6-7)
C. *Nine Paradoxes of the Worker* (verses 8-10)

A. *Nine Testings of the Worker* (verses 4-5)

But in all things approving ourselves as the ministers of God, in much patience, in afflictions, in necessities, in distresses, in stripes, in imprisonments, in tumults, in labours, in watchings, in fastings.

This will ordinarily be read to show ten testings, but patience is in fact, the thing to be developed in the worker. It is the object of the testings. The nine things which follow are the means by which patience is developed.

1. In Afflictions

Affliction does not seem to have any compatible place in God's affection for us, but it is there. It is there as a part of the curriculum of patience.

2. In Necessities

These are needs unsupplied. Is not this in contradiction to the statement, "My God shall supply all your need"? In a sense it is, but when you place it as a part of the classroom of patience, then it is not. It is for a higher purpose that God sometimes withholds. There is a higher purpose in grace than merely granting contentment. Character does not grow out of gratification. To withhold is sometimes more beneficial than to bestow.

3. In Distresses

These are those compressing experiences that put us into straits. We get into the narrows of confining circumstances and then wonder why. It is to develop what would not come in another way.

4. In Stripes

These are man-made testings. This particular kind which puts a whip to the bared back is foreign to us, but early Christians knew what stripes meant. Paul bore the raised welts of terrible beatings. He felt the stinging lash of a pagan whip.

5. In Imprisonments

These follow stripes, for having been beaten, the victim was thrown into prison for confinement and further abuse.

6. In Tumults

This was mob violence and the oppression which came from street crowds incited to inflammatory hatred by bigoted religious leaders.

7. In Labors

This was toil. Paul was a tentmaker and plied his trade with vigor to supply himself with means to carry on his work for Christ. Real Christian service is arduous labor. It knows no hours and brings a weariness to mind and body.

8. In Watchings

These were nights of sleeplessness. They were night vigils caused by an agonized heart. A mind working overtime considering and planning, found no rest in sleep.

9. In Fastings

Here is self-denial and sacrifice. It was the rigorous training of body and soul for the difficult tasks of service. It was hunger and thirst willingly endured that the message might be taken to those who had not heard.

What testings these were! How they must have tried every nerve and fiber of body and soul. They were the testings of patience. Whoever is willing to pay their price can have their profit.

An old saying tells us what is sauce for the goose is sauce for the gander. Likewise, what is good for the people is good for the preacher. The preacher finds himself constantly chagrined and challenged by the Bible he endeavors to preach and teach to others. It is a constant source of personal measurement.

Following Paul through the maze of his experiences, the preacher stands ashamed that he has been so unwilling to take the hard way. He has often found himself selfishly saying that he would not do certain things because it meant difficulty. In the face of Paul's experiences he blushes for shame. The easy way is unworthy of any real servant of Christ. He must forswear the past and declare a new future.

It is natural to want the easy way. We unconsciously choose it. Colonel Lawrence of Arabia told of two Arab chieftains who had been brought to London by the British Government. It was a good-will gesture to win their allegiance to the British cause in the Near East. They had been given many honors and entertained with lavish luxuriance. As they were about to return to Arabia, Colonel Lawrence asked what they would like to take back with them as a typical memento of their visit. One of them quickly replied, ''We would like to have two hot water faucets to take home with us. It would be nice in Arabia to turn them on and have hot water any time one wished.''

Of course, they saw the easy side of hot water. It was the bright and shiny faucet. Back of that faucet were pipes and valves and reservoirs and fire. Without the fire the faucet was of no use.

Many of us would like the convenient gadgets of godliness. We like to gather our religion on the run and enjoy ourselves. That is the easy way. Back of all true godliness there is consecration; consecration means fire and fire means purging and pressure. We can wish for the nice shiny faucets of religious ecstasy, but the service that the faucet represents means fire.

B. *Nine Characteristics of the Worker* (verses 6-7)

By pureness, by knowledge, by longsuffering, by kindness, by the Holy Ghost, by love unfeigned, by the word of truth, by the power of God, by the armour of righteousness on the right hand and on the left.

The previous nine testings were what the worker found outside. These nine characteristics are what the worker should find inside. They are not to be merely artificial religious equipment, but actual life attainments. They are to represent character and to reflect the man inside.

If previously we were shown the lengths required to develop patience, we are now shown how this patience is to be manifested. So often we manifest petulance instead of patience. Before it was the experience in which we were to live. Now it is the characteristics by which we are to live.

1. By Pureness

The greatest personal credential of the worker is his personal purity of character and conduct, not his brilliance or his ability. We have laid altogether too much stress on what a man does without a proportionate emphasis on what a man is.

This is listed first because God desires and requires pureness first. We study to be wise; let us also study to be good and right and so transparently pure of life that offense will not be given.

2. By Knowledge

There is an old Greek maxim which said: "The beginning of knowledge is the knowledge of ignorance." He who knows everything in his own eyes, really knows nothing.

God cannot fill what is already full. An emptying must come before there can be a filling.

Here, knowledge has particular reference to spiritual

illumination. A Christian worker should be proficient in a wide sphere but there is one sphere where he must be particularly efficient. He must have spiritual insight. He may become acquainted with a wide range of subjects, but his primary field is not economics or psychology; it is spiritual understanding and guidance.

God pity the Christian minister today who knows more about newspapers, magazines and best sellers than he knows about the Bible! It is this Book which is our hope and we must become spiritual specialists of the soul.

There is a medicine of the soul which we have to dispense to a world afflicted with the nervous disorders of the soul. This medicine is done up in capsules of Bible verses. It is for internal application. It is not a gaudy philosophic cosmetic smeared upon the surface to give an attractive appearance. It is a therapy for the soul. Such a message we must give and God forbid that we be guilty of malpractice.

3. By Long-suffering

This is long-suffering under ill treatment. It is a forbearance that endures. It is the refusal to be provoked. It is courtesy under criticism.

Here is a grace of universal need. Its display is a fine test of the advance we have made in our growth in grace.

4. By Kindness

There is no misunderstanding the meaning of this. Kindness will win where the finest rhetoric will fail. Kindness melts the ice of indifference and breaks the flinty heart. It is the best introduction we can give to the message we have.

5. By the Holy Ghost

This does not refer to our use of the Holy Ghost as some kind of religious tool, yet that is the idea which many hold. Many think the Holy Ghost is an emergency instrument. Christian service is His use and employment of us. Service is the fruit of His blessing and power in our lives.

There is something greater than being filled with the presence of God. It is expressing and exhibiting the fruits of His indwelling.

This will give a true and proper holiness of life. It has been well said that "holiness has been preached so much that it has become a synonym for hollowness." We have spoiled a good thing by dwelling on a name. The indwelling Holy Spirit will produce a holiness of great attraction.

6. By Love Unfeigned

This means sincere love. There is a pretended love which tarnishes. Here is an unaffected love which endures and lasts and wears extremely well.

7. By the Word of Truth.

This is the word of the Scriptures. It is our stock in trade. It is our commodity of character. It is not only the weapon of offense, but also the armor of defense.

8. By the Power of God

This means God's power in us. It is not God's power in the sun or in the wind or the laws of nature, but rather in the laws of the spiritual life within. It is God's power reduced to the familiar terms of human necessities. It is wonderful to think of God's power in creation, but this is God's power in His new creation. It is God's power in heart, life, home and business.

9. By the Armor of Righteousness

It was to be on the right hand and on the left. In the right hand was the sword of the Spirit which is the Word of God. This was for our offensive warfare. On the left hand was the shield of faith which was for our defensive warfare. There must be both a sword and a shield.

The Scriptures speak of three kinds of armor for three kinds of foe. We face the threefold foe of the world, the flesh and the devil.

There is the armor of righteousness referred to here in order that we may fight the foe which is of the world.

There is the armor of light referred to in Romans 13:12 in order that we may fight the foe which is the flesh.

Then there is the armor of God referred to in Ephesians 6:11 in order that we may fight the foe which is the devil.

Thus the soul is fully armored for its necessities.

Sometimes we try desperately to reconcile certain of our experiences with justice and with Scripture. It is often impossible because Christian experience has its paradoxes. There can be no reconciliation to sight; only to faith. There are contradictions that will always contradict. There are paradoxes that will always be paradoxical.

We are thrown back time after time upon a statement in this epistle, "We walk by faith, not by sight." By faith, a paradox does not become more understandable, but it does become a part of the picture that completes the whole. There are some things which we will never fully understand while there are others that work out to glorious conclusions before our wondering eyes.

C. *Nine Paradoxes of the Worker* (verses 8-10)

By honour and dishonour, by evil report and good report: as deceivers, and yet true; as unknown, and yet well known; as dying, and,

behold, we live; as chastened, and not killed; as sorrowful, yet alway
rejoicing; as poor, yet making many rich; as having nothing, and yet
possessing all things.

1. By Honor and Dishonor

From some come honor and praise, while from others
come dishonor and infamy. Some will approve your
work and others will disapprove. How can you reconcile the two? You cannot, so do not try. Go on, without
being elated over your honor nor deflated over your
dishonor.

2. By Evil Report and Good Report

On the one hand a worker is met with praise and on
the other hand with calumny. One upholds him, another
debases him. One credits him with good motives while
another defames his character.

We must learn to balance these reports so as not to
be dependent on the one nor despondent over the other.
Remember, men may bandy your reputation about, but
they cannot touch your character. It is character that
will count in the long run.

3. As Deceivers and Yet True

Here is the paradox of being branded as a deceiver but
vindicated as true. We must not read into this that it
is as an actual deceiver that one extends the cause of
Christ. Rather, it means that even though some may
slander you with the epithet of a deceiver, you will be
vindicated as being true by continuing to be His servant
in sincerity and simplicity. The best vindication is
your life.

4. As Unknown and Yet Well Known

This refers to the obscurity into which true Christian
character often passes in the world. "The world will
little note nor long remember" its greatest souls. A
man is well known in the world because of his public

relationship, yet his position alone is not always the measurement of true greatness.

There are in our times well-established aristocracies. There is the aristocracy of wealth in which men can have prominence because of their money. There is the aristocracy of blood in which men are prominent because of their ancestry. Then there is the aristocracy of position in which men have gained recognition through place. These are only transient categories.

There is still another aristocracy that belongs to eternity. It is the aristocracy of the twice-born. It elevates one to a place of great blessing and inheritance.

What does it matter then if you are ignored by men so long as you are recognized by God? What does it matter if men depreciate so long as God appreciates? What does it matter if men forget so long as God remembers?

5. As Dying and Behold We Live

Facing death's constant and imminent danger there is the deliverance of God's daily providences.

Here was a remarkable testimony of life in the midst of danger. Surely this was dangerous living, but it was also glorious living. There is too much delicate living in our day. There is too little disposition to venture all in the cause we serve.

6. As Chastened and Not Killed

This was not a sheltered life, free from the blasts of adversity and the perils of ordinary existence. It was all-out devotion to a great cause and a mighty leader.

7. As Sorrowful and Yet Alway Rejoicing

Here was an evidence of an inner triumph that put tears to flight by the smiles of praise. Who dares to rejoice in sorrow? A fanatic? A lunatic? Must one be

totally devoid of all sense of reason and be so emotion-
ally unstable and so reckless as to actually laugh in the
face of disaster? This is not hysteria. It is the Christian's way to reconcile the paradoxes of life. It is
balancing the budget of experience. It is putting faith
into the blackout of sight.

8. As Poor, Yet Making Many Rich

We have all sighed for the riches of gold when we
might have been wealthy with the riches of God. There
are more kinds of wealth than the credit of money.

"Money may purchase the husk of many things, but
not the kernel of anything. It can buy food, but not the
appetite with which to eat that food. It can buy medicine, but not health. It can buy acquaintances, but not
friends. It can buy servants, but not faithfulness. It
can buy pleasure, but not happiness" (Ibsen).

It is possible to make many rich without having a
dollar to one's credit. You can bestow the riches of
happiness, salvation, peace and joy. Let us begin to
enjoy the paradox of poverty.

9. As Having Nothing, and Yet Possessing All Things

There are those who own many things and yet possess
nothing. They are possessed by what they have. They
are controlled, body, mind and soul by their possessions.
They are slaves to the master Money.

There is still another class who have nothing, yet
possess all things.

Ministers must forswear the ambitions of other men.
They must surrender their right to high places and
large fortunes which others enjoy. Yet, without these
they are not without possessions. Theirs is a possession
of spirit which makes them rich in the things that do not
perish.

So it is with all disciples of Christ, that in the pursuit of the better things we come into possession of "an inheritance incorruptible, and undefiled, and that fadeth not away, reserved in heaven for you."

Let us not despise wealth, for with it we can bless the world. Rather, let us learn to appreciate spiritual wealth, for it is greater than all other forms of possession.

The position which a Christian holds in the world by virtue of his profession is as important as the profession. It matters little what kind of a profession we make if our position does not support it. Our profession is intended to proclaim our position, while our position is meant to ratify our profession.

III. Life's Associations (verses 11-18)

A twofold association is referred to here. It is the believer in his relation to other believers and also in his relation to unbelievers. The strategy by which Satan seeks to destroy God's work in us and through us, is manifold. He seeks the outright pollution of truth in some cases. In others he seeks to pollute Christian relations with worldly alliances. It is this thing which is discussed in the next immediate verses.

A. *The Believer's Affection for Believers* (verses 11-13)

O ye Corinthians, our mouth is open unto you, our heart is enlarged. Ye are not straitened in us, but ye are straitened in your own bowels. Now for a recompence in the same, (I speak as unto my children,) be ye also enlarged.

Paul made an earnest plea for the full and complete affection of the Corinthians. He said a very necessary thing—a thing which needs to be said with emphasis today. It was his desire to have the undiluted affection of the Corinthian believers. To them he had spoken frankly. Nothing was hid from them. He exposed the innermost secrets of his soul. Now, he pleaded for a return in kind. He asked for their love and good will. He bid for their fidelity.

The solidarity of Christians is not achieved by all believing the same things. Doctrinal unanimity must be followed by fraternal unity. We must not only believe the same things, but love in the same way.

Paul understood that if Christ's cause was to be extended into the vast areas of paganism, it must begin with a body of Christians who loved each other.

B. *The Believer's Alliance with Unbelievers* (verses 14-18)

Be ye not unequally yoked together with unbelievers: for what fellowship hath righteousness with unrighteousness? and what communion hath light with darkness? And what concord hath Christ with Belial? or what part hath he that believeth with an infidel? And what agreement hath the temple of God with idols? for ye are the temple of the living God; as God hath said, I will dwell in them, and walk in them; and I will be their God, and they shall be my people. Wherefore come out from among them, and be ye separate, saith the Lord, and touch not the unclean thing; and I will receive you, and will be a Father unto you, and ye shall be my sons and daughters, saith the Lord Almighty.

This sets forth a very important principle of Christian practice and behavior. It is not creating a set of religious taboos, nor is it laying down the law. It is a clear statement of principle which is to govern the Christian as he walks on this earth.

In the first place, it speaks of two separate spheres of life based upon the Christian concept of life. That concept is clearly stated in chapter 5 verse 17: "Therefore if any man be in Christ, he is a new creature: old things are passed away; behold, all things are become new." One sphere is in Christ and the other sphere is out of Christ. One is the sphere of old things and the other the sphere of new things. One is the sphere of the Christian and the other the sphere of the world. It is exceedingly important to understand this conception of life, for it will affect the whole course of our Christian conduct.

The Christian who belongs to the sphere of new things is to think and act and live in keeping with that sphere. He is not to be shuttling back and forth between one and the other. If he does, he will be destroying both his experience and his influence.

When a Christian understands this, his life will take on new meaning and importance. He will see himself as one who belongs to Christ for high and holy things. It will be something more than a legalistic regulation of his life. Instead, it will be the high purpose of living for the best and noblest things.

There was an important reason why this should have to be true of the Corinthians. The world of their day was wholly idolatrous. To have followed Christ out of that kind of a world meant a clear break. One could not be half Christian and half pagan. It required a clean-cut separation.

There is also an important reason why it should be true of modern Christians. The entire scheme of Christian experience is based on a new life. It is something more than a religious profession. Christianity is not a better human life. It is not something that seeks to improve the present world life. It is a new life that moves in a new sphere. Because this is so, we are warned not to lose our identity in the world. We are to maintain our intercourse in the world socially, commercially and professionally without making common cause with the world system.

The world system and the Christian system are two separate and distinct operations. One springs from the material realm and the other from the spiritual. One is controlled by the mastership of Satan and the other by the mastership of Christ. One is conducive to the flesh and the other to the spirit.

For this reason we are cautioned and warned, "Be ye not unequally yoked together with unbelievers." The yoke would be unequal because it would link the new and the old.

Five questions are propounded to reveal how unequal this yoking of the new and the old would be.

1. "What fellowship hath righteousness with unrighteousness?"
2. "What communion hath light with darkness?"
3. "What concord hath Christ with Belial?"
4. "What part hath he that believeth with an infidel?"
5. "What agreement hath the temple of God with idols?"

Here are two kingdoms of truth and two spheres of life.

One kingdom is described by the terms righteousness, light, Christ, believer and the temple of God. The other kingdom is described by the words unrighteousness, darkness, Belial, infidel and idols.

These two kingdoms are so different and diverse that the Scriptures declare that between them there can be neither fellowship, communion, concord, part or agreement. These words which the Scriptures employ indicate how impossible it is for the Christian to live in both spheres and retain his distinction. Any attempt to do so will cause a loss of personal blessing and influence.

Everything in this world tends to revert unless protected by separation. To obtain the best roses they must be separated by grafting and cultivation. If allowed to grow by themselves, they revert to scrawny and unlovely blooms. Likewise the new life implanted in us must be protected and nurtured by the principle of separation. It must be lived in the sphere of new things. If we feed it on the things of the old life, it will starve and become ineffectual and we will revert to the old way of life.

Therefore we hear the injunction, "Come out from among them, and be ye separate, saith the Lord." This separation does not mean segregation. To live a separated life does not mean that we have to segregate ourselves from the world. One may move among one's fellow men in all the necessary and proper social, professional and commercial contacts but still retain his identity and integrity as a Christian. One can live in one sphere and still be living by the other sphere. One can walk in the world and still walk as a Christian.

There is a reward for this kind of Christian walking and living. It is a closer alliance with God. He promises us the intimate fellowship of a father and the lavish personal blessings that such a relationship brings.

7

THE LIFE THAT ENDURES CHASTENING
2 Corinthians 7

At this point it is well to remember that we have in this Second Epistle to the Corinthians a biographical record of its writer. He has given a simple account of his own experiences. They add up to the grand total of godliness. They reveal the simplicity of the Christian faith. They show how the ordinary events of ordinary people may be made into a noble pattern of life.

This chapter speaks of the lives of Christians in four ways.

   I.   THE CLEANSED LIFE (verse 1)
  II.   THE CONVERTED LIFE (verses 2-4)
 III.   THE CHASTENED LIFE (verses 5-12)
 IV.   THE COMFORTED LIFE (verses 13-16)

I.   THE CLEANSED LIFE (verse 1)

Having therefore these promises, dearly beloved, let us cleanse ourselves from all filthiness of the flesh and spirit, perfecting holiness in the fear of God.

The promises referred to in this verse go back to the previous chapter in which the Christian was challenged to live a separated life. In living such a life he would experience the presence and blessing of God in a very marked manner. The promise was, "Wherefore come out from among them, and be ye separate, saith the Lord, and touch not the unclean thing; and I will receive

you, and will be a Father unto you, and ye shall be my
sons and daughters, saith the Lord Almighty."

You will notice this promise is conditional. If we will
come out from evil alliances, God will come unto us in
intimate blessing and power. If we will walk with God
in separation, God will walk with us in greater blessing.
In other words, if we will obey the laws of the spiritual
life, we shall receive the profit of such obedience.

This refers to the responsibility which is the Christian's with regard to his own development and advancement in character and life. There can be no progress
outwardly until there is cleansing and correction inwardly. Christian experience begins within.

The basis for all experience is found in the Scriptures.
Here it is specifically stated as "these promises." And
"these promises" hold out to every Christian a noble
ideal. It is the ideal of a life lived in the close companionship of God. It is life freed from the dragging
liabilities of evil alliances.

On the basis of God's Word we are charged to do two
things.

A. *Negatively*—"let us cleanse ourselves from all
filthiness of the flesh and spirit."

There are two kinds of cleansing. One is positional
and the other is practical. Our positional cleansing is
something which only God can do. It is inward and can
only be done by the grace of God. Our practical cleansing is outward. It is something each of us is charged
with. It is the cleansing of our actions, our deeds and
our words.

We are too prone to pray for God to cleanse us when
there is much that depends upon us. The words here are
very plain "let us cleanse ourselves." If there is in us at
this moment a known sin or an unchristian habit, its
cleansing is our responsibility. While only God can

cleanse us from the moral pollution of sin, we can cleanse ourselves from the habitual practice of sins.

This cleansing of ourselves is to include two spheres.

1. Filthiness of the Flesh

These are the sins of our bodily members. They are the sins of the five physical senses. They belong to the physical part of us and include any practice, habit or indulgence which will cause uncleanness or defilement.

Filthiness is something that soils and whatever soils us is wrong. It should be put away. It is not a question of whether it is conventional, but whether it is Christian. Christianity stands for all that is clean. Any habit, practice or indulgence of the physical senses that soils us and causes uncleanness, is wrong and therefore unchristian. Concerning it, we have a very definite responsibility—cleanse ourselves.

2. Filthiness of the Spirit

Previously, it was sins of the flesh. Here it is the sins of the disposition. Before it was the outer man, here it is the inner man.

One may be scrupulously Christian in habit but very decidedly unchristian in disposition. A person may neither smoke, drink, be immoral or guilty of the violent pollutions of the flesh yet be most unattractive in his nature.

This filthiness of the spirit refers to hatred, malice, jealousy, animosity, ill-temper, pride and a host of companion evils.

It is not enough to cleanse ourselves of defiling habits. There are defiling traits of character. One can defile and soil home life by a selfish disposition. He can spoil the lives and peace of other people by a contentious and troublesome spirit.

There is just as much reason to be clean in spirit as

to be clean in body. There should be as much evidence of Christ in our disposition as there is in our activities. Unless Christ has made us more agreeable and more sociable and more decent to live with, we have not experienced the fullest measure of His grace.

All of this, remember, is something which is put squarely up to us. It says, "Let us cleanse ourselves." Do not wait for God to do what He expects you to do. Do not sit around piously wishing to be someone better than you are, but get up in the strength of Christ and become that better person. Do not wish to do what you must will to do. An old Chinese proverb says, "Great souls have wills; feeble ones have only wishes."

Here is your responsibility. The Bible is your challenge. Christ is your master. The Holy Spirit is your strength.

B. *Positively*—"perfecting holiness in the fear of God."

Once again we find ourselves faced with a great responsibility. We are charged with the responsibility of perfecting holiness. Many of us have considered that to be a passive work of grace. We have said, with a great deal of spiritual laziness, that holiness is something God will do for us. That is as true in one sense as was true of moral cleansing. There is both a positional holiness and a practical holiness. What we are before God in our standing, is by His grace, but what we are before man in our state, is by our own determination. The first is by God's will and the second by our will. The holiness of our standing will only become the holiness of our state as we yield to the means of grace which God provides for our growth.

One thing is eternally certain. There can be no perfecting of holiness unless there is a cleansing of filthiness. Filthiness recedes as holiness proceeds. Filthiness goes out as holiness comes in. Even so, holiness is not merely the absence of filthiness. It is not the state of religious vacuum. It is not what is left when you have removed the filthiness of flesh and spirit. Instead, it is the indwelling Spirit. It is the increasing stature of Christ. Holiness is, in fact, the very life of Christ. So long as that life is stifled by filthiness, it cannot grow. Give it room and area by cleansing what is foreign to it and it will grow and increase. This is holiness. It is the life of Christ making holy the life of the Christian.

This cleansing and perfecting is to be accomplished by faith and in fear. Be careful to notice that it says in fear and not by fear. It is something which is done by faith while we have a reverent respect for God. Whoever lives reverently before God will find its effect in life. The fear of God is not fright but such reverence and regard for God as will cause us to want to be what He desires. The person who properly fears God is one who has cleansed himself from the spoiling defilements of life and is perfecting a holy character.

Take God out of life and men live to no good or intelligent purpose. It is this very fact that makes so much of our modern life evil and senseless.

Having God in life is something more than believing in a supreme being. A person may believe in such a being and still be as pagan as a Roman.

There is a difference between belief and faith. Many people believe in God who do not have faith in God. One is simply an attitude of mind while the other is an act of will. One may believe in the necessity of food, but believing does not supply the body with nourishment. One must act on that belief and take food into the body before belief is of any practical value.

So it is with one's belief and faith in God. You may believe that God is necessary to your life, but until your faith acts upon your belief, God will be no practical part of your life.

Belief in God requires a conception whereas faith in God requires a decision. Belief results in a conclusion; faith results in a conversion. It is conversion which puts God into life.

It was this fact of conversion in the lives of his Corinthian friends in which Paul rejoiced.

II. The Converted Life (verses 2-4)

Receive us; we have wronged no man, we have corrupted no man, we have defrauded no man. I speak not this to condemn you: for I have said before, that ye are in our hearts to die and live with you. Great is my boldness of speech toward you, great is my glorying of you: I am filled with comfort, I am exceeding joyful in all our tribulations.

Here is an intimate touch of Christian fellowship. How natural it was for Paul to desire the fellowship of the Corinthians. He asked them to receive him. There were some who had sought to spoil this fellowship by traducing Paul's character, therefore he reminded them of his careful life. He had not wronged any one; had not defrauded any one; he had been careful to live so as not to injure others, and consequently merited the most intimate fellowship and approval of his fellow Christians.

Paul did not say these things in condemnation of the Corinthians. He had spoken of them in highest terms. He had boasted of the work of grace that had taken place in Corinth. As a matter of fact, so great was his confidence in the converted lives of his Corinthian friends that he declared himself as determined to live and die for them.

This kind of loyalty is refreshing. It was loyalty based on the new order of life. That order was the new life of conversion. It was the result of the new creation. The old paganism had given way to the new Christianity. The old lasciviousness had gone and a new righteousness had come. Here was a solid basis for confidence and fellowship.

No matter what age we may live in, the greatest need is for converted lives. The solution of our problems, according to Jesus, is in the transformation of character. "The human drama is not playing itself out very well, and no shifting of the scenery can fix the drama up. Something profound must happen to the actors if it is to come out right." That "something profound" is the profound necessity of conversion.

For this reason the Gospel plan of life is indispensable to our day and to our social order. "Christianity is not a cosmetic to adorn the spiritual externals of our society. It is the medicine which can cure the inner wrongness that ruins life." This is so because conversion goes to the root of the human wrong, which is sin.

If the Bible's idea of sin is right, then we are equally sure its idea of the remedy for sin is right. If it is true that men are born sinners, then we will find it true that men must be born again. Sin is something associated with a first birth and salvation is something associated with a second birth.

Discipline is an important part of discipleship. An undisciplined disciple will find himself an unprepared, undeveloped and unfit disciple. Without discipline there can never be conspicuous Christianity.

Today we find ourselves in the midst of an undisciplined Christianity. In the first century Christianity was unpopular and the disciples suffered unmentionable persecution, but the discipline of those days gave the Church a triumphant life. Today Christianity is popular. The Christian is scarcely distinguishable from the non-Christian. There is no discipline in his life. There is none from without and none from within and in consequence he is soft and ineffectual.

The disciplined Christian is the one who follows Christ all the way. This is a Christ-given and self-chosen distinction in habits and activities. He determines to mark himself by what he does and does not do. This is not legalism; it is loyalty. It is not narrow-mindedness; it is Christianity at its best. Jesus said, "If any man will come after me, let him deny himself, and take up his cross, and follow me. For whosoever will save his life shall lose it: and whosoever will lose his life for my sake shall find it" (Matthew 16:24-25). That is discipline.

Denial is not indulgence. Following Jesus is not following the world. Finding one's life is not spending it or squandering it on the whims of selfishness. Following Christ means disciplined discipleship.

The danger of an undisciplined life is sin in the life. It happened to one at Corinth.

III. The Chastened Life (verses 5-12)

Two experiences are related in this section of the chapter.

A. *The Apostle's Experience with Adversity*
(verse 5)

For, when we were come into Macedonia, our flesh had no rest,
but we were troubled on every side; without were fightings, within
were fears.

Here is a common pattern of experience. It is outward foes and inward fears. The flesh is the arena of
suffering. With Paul it was an endless succession of
bitter conflicts centered around him. He was constantly
troubled and hindered by these distressing afflictions.
His fears were inner concerns and they represent an
experience common to any Christian. We all have conflicts of one kind or another. We all have our fears
and concerns. We find ourselves fretfully wondering
how things will go.

To say that this is not a fact, is just plain dishonesty.
It is better to admit it and plan for its defeat than to
try piously to avoid the issue.

Of one thing you may be sure, Paul did not succumb
to his fears. He may have experienced them, but he
was not conquered by them. Fear was conquered by
faith.

There is always a good use for adversity. The fightings and fears of Paul were the means of making a better
Paul. If we would recognize this, then we would take
a different attitude to the adversities we suffer.

B. *The Corinthians' Experience with Chastening*
(verses 6-12)

Nevertheless God, that comforteth those that are cast down, comforted us by the coming of Titus; and not by his coming only, but
by the consolation wherewith he was comforted in you, when he told
us your earnest desire, your mourning, your fervent mind toward
me; so that I rejoiced the more. For though I made you sorry with

a letter, I do not repent, though I did repent: for I perceive that the same epistle hath made you sorry, though it were but for a season. Now I rejoice, not that ye were made sorry, but that ye sorrowed to repentance: for ye were made sorry after a godly manner, that ye might receive damage by us in nothing. For godly sorrow worketh repentance to salvation not to be repented of: but the sorrow of the world worketh death. For behold this selfsame thing, that ye sorrowed after a godly sort, what carefulness it wrought in you, yea, what clearing of yourselves, yea, what indignation, yea, what fear, yea, what vehement desire, yea, what zeal, yea, what revenge! In all things ye have approved yourselves to be clear in this matter. Wherefore, though I wrote unto you, I did it not for his cause that had done the wrong, nor for his cause that suffered wrong, but that our care for you in the sight of God might appear unto you.

The incident referred to was the case of sinners who had crept into the Corinthian church. Paul had rebuked the sin and required that the sinners be punished. When Titus returned to Paul from Corinth and reported that this discipline had been administered it brought him no little comfort. He was pleased with their faithful obedience, but he was also pleased with their determination to be clean. They had been courageous enough to judge evil and put it away. Not until that is true of all of us will we be ready to inherit the blessings God has promised His people.

IV. THE COMFORTED LIFE (verses 13-16)

Therefore we were comforted in your comfort: yea, and exceedingly the more joyed we for the joy of Titus, because his spirit was refreshed by you all. For if I have boasted any thing to him of you, I am not ashamed; but as we spake all things to you in truth, even so our boasting, which I made before Titus, is found a truth. And his inward affection is more abundant toward you, whilst he remembereth the obedience of you all, how with fear and trembling ye received him. I rejoice therefore that I have confidence in you in all things.

An unpleasant situation had ended very fortunately. Paul found comfort out of the comfort of his friends. He had invested very heavily in them. He had invested his effort and concern. He had invested prayer and agony. Now it was beginning to pay dividends.

All the misgivings of former days were gone. Paul now came to the satisfaction of a great confidence. He concluded with these words, "I rejoice therefore that I have confidence in you in all things."

Confidence is something to be coveted by all. God bring each of us speedily to the day when it can be said of us, "I rejoice therefore that I have confidence in you in all things."

Section II

THE MINISTRATIONS OF THE CHRISTIAN

2 Corinthians 8—9

8

THE CHRISTIAN'S PRACTICE OF CHARITY

2 Corinthians 8

Ignorant men have complained that the Bible leaves people up in the clouds of impractical religious piety and that Christianity is an empty hymn-singing display of religious theory. In the face of this it is interesting to notice how the Bible addresses itself to practical things and how it makes Christianity a thing of the hands and the feet as well as of the heart, the head and the lips.

This chapter deals with the practice of Christian charity in three particulars.

    I. CHRISTIAN CHARITY AS A GRACE OF LIFE (verses 1-8)
    II. CHRISTIAN CHARITY BY THE EXAMPLE OF CHRIST (verses 9-15)
    III. CHRISTIAN CHARITY THROUGH EFFICIENT ADMINISTRATION (verses 16-24)

I. CHRISTIAN CHARITY AS A GRACE OF LIFE (verses 1-8)

Giving is a grace. It was urged upon the Corinthians by the example of the Macedonians. Paul had been in this Macedonian area and was on his way to Jerusalem. He had just met Titus who brought him the good news about Corinth. Since Paul was soon to be in Corinth he sent this letter in advance in order that they might be prepared for their duties in connection with their social obligations.

The occasion for this giving was the need of the Jewish
Christians at Jerusalem. They had passed through
bitter persecution which had swept away their homes
and their means of employment. They were now desti-
tute and in desperate need of the assistance which was
due them from fellow Christians. It was this urgent
need that Paul was laying before the Corinthians.

In seeking to stir them up to a proper effort, he referred to the sacrifices of the Christians in Macedonia.

This is often necessary in connection with our own
giving. We think we are generous, liberal and sacri-
ficial until we behold the giving of others.

A business man and a lawyer, both Christians, were
traveling in Korea. One day they saw in the field by
the side of the road a young man pulling a rude plow,
while an old man held the handles. The lawyer was
amused and took a snapshot of the scene. "That's a
curious picture! I suppose they are very poor," he
said to the missionary who was interpreter and guide
to the party. "Yes," was the quiet reply. "That is the
family of Chi Boui. When the church was being built
they were eager to give something to it, but they had no
money, so they sold their only ox and gave the money
to the church. This spring they are pulling the plow
themselves." The lawyer and the business man by his
side were silent for some moments. Then the business
man said, "That must have been a real sacrifice." "They
did not call it that," said the missionary. "They
thought it was fortunate that they had the ox to sell."
The lawyer and the business man had not much to say.
When they reached home the lawyer took the picture
to his minister and told him about it. "I want to double
my pledge to the church," he said. "Give me some
plow work, please. I have never yet given anything to
my church that cost me anything."

The giving of these Macedonians, which is cited for

the emulation of the Corinthians and us, is described
in a threefold sense.

A.   *It Was Under Adversity* (verses 1-2)

> Moreover, brethren, we do you to wit of the grace of God bestowed
> on the churches of Macedonia; how that in a great trial of affliction
> the abundance of their joy and their deep poverty abounded unto the
> riches of their liberality.

Let us study the expressions in this verse.

1. Abundant Joy in Great Affliction

In spite of the great trial of their affliction they had
an abundance of joy. It was not a case of enduring their
affliction with a grim patience and a dogged endurance.
It was an overrunning joy in the midst of great affliction.

This is the mark of great grace. It points to the development of Christian experience beyond the ordinary
run of discipleship. It was more than being religious.
It was being victoriously Christian.

2. Rich Liberality in Deep Poverty

We notice these Macedonians gave as they could and
what they could. They gave according to their present
ability and did not wait until they became affluent. Whoever waits for abundance before giving, will never give
at all. Those who give in the times of poverty will also
give in the times of abundance. Those who never give
in the times of adversity will never give in the times of
prosperity.

The Macedonians' poverty became the occasion for
their liberality. By liberality, it does not necessarily
mean large sums, but a sum proportionate to their ability. We estimate giving by the size of the gift, whereas
God estimates it by the size of the balance. It was so
in the case of the poor widow who "cast more in," Jesus
said, "than all they [the rich] which have cast into the
treasury," for the widow's was "all her living."

B. *It Was Spontaneous* (verses 3-4)

For to their power, I bear record, yea, and beyond their power
they were willing of themselves; praying us with much intreaty that
we would receive the gift, and take upon us the fellowship of the
ministering to the saints.

The grace of giving is not according to compulsion.
It is something spontaneous, genuine and sincere. This
was the case with the Macedonians. They gave of their
own accord. When they gave they did not measure
their gift according to their ability. They gave more
than they comfortably could afford. They gave beyond
the limits of their ability.

Furthermore, we notice, they insisted on giving. It
was not given with reluctance and hesitancy but with
prayerful entreaty. They implored Paul to receive their
gift and pass it on in the spirit of Christian fellowship.

Many times we make praying the substitute for paying.
It is so easy to say, "I am praying for you," and make
our prayers a substitute for the discharge of our legitimate obligations. Prayers for the sick are fine and in
order, but they are worth nothing when we try to make
them a substitute for visiting the sick. We should never
cease praying, but it is no release from doing something
for someone in need. Neither is prayer a substitute for
giving financial assistance when such assistance is within our power to give.

The Macedonians sent prayer with their gifts and
did not merely offer prayer as a substitute for their
gifts. They prayed and paid. They accompanied prayer
with the practical evidence of faith.

When we observe these Macedonians we realize that
poverty is never an excuse nor is prayer a substitute
for doing what we can in the material assistance of
others.

C. *It Was in Self-Surrender* (verse 5)

And this they did, not as we hoped, but first gave their own selves to the Lord, and unto us by the will of God.

The secret of their giving was in themselves. It was their own complete consecration and self-surrender. Having given themselves it was easy to give their means. In fact, what we have is what we are. Our substance is ourselves. When we make a surrender of ourselves we also surrender our substance.

Proper Christian giving is never an impersonal matter. It is a sacred surrender of one's self. When we give in the proper sense we give what we are with what we have.

We notice further, that this sort of giving was "by the will of God." When our will parallels God's will, giving has reached its highest height. It is regulated not by our whims, but by His will. So much of our giving is by whim that there is a lack of means for God's work. If we lived in the will of God and gave accordingly, there would be ample means for the cause of Christ. How sad it is that this is not true.

A man of great learning and perception once remarked, "Ask yonder sun, 'What art thou doing?' and he will answer, 'The will of God.' Ask those waves of the ocean and they will answer, 'The will of God.' Turn to the tiny flower drinking in the dew, 'What art thou doing?' and it will answer, 'The will of God.' "

Man, highest of God's creation, listen to me: What art thou doing? Is not the answer this: "What I choose; I please myself; I do as I will and assert my independence of God as though He were not"?

The purpose of citing the example of the Macedonians in the matter of giving was to incite the Corinthians to the same spirit and action. Paul said, "Insomuch that we desired Titus, that as he had begun, so he would also finish in you the same grace also'' (verse 6).

Paul was further anxious that their lives would not lack a complete furnishing in the Christian graces. ''Therefore as ye abound in every thing, in faith, and utterance, and knowledge, and in all diligence, and in your love to us, see that ye abound in this grace also'' (verse 7). They had faith, utterance, knowledge, diligence and love. And to these should be added the grace of giving.

The grace of giving completes the graces of Christian character. This is so because giving is the outflow of the inflow of grace. It is faith in action. It is utterance made real. It is knowledge made practical. It is diligence applied. It is love in its finest form. In these ways, giving completes the graces of the Christian life and makes faith the most practical thing in the world.

II. Christian Charity by the Example of Christ
(verses 9-15)

Having appealed to the example of the impoverished Macedonians, Paul now appealed to the example set by the Master, Jesus Christ.

He spoke of five things.

A. *Grace in Giving* (verse 9a)

For ye know the grace of our Lord Jesus Christ.

The incentive in giving is not the compulsion of a commandment but the sincerity of love. In fact, giving will prove the sincerity of our love.

If giving is a grace, it could not be a law, therefore, when we think of Christian giving we are thinking of something different from Jewish giving. In the Old Testament, the Jew gave a tithe because it was the law. In the New Testament, the Christian gives apart from the law. To insist on the tithe because it is law, is to insist on something which does not belong in the sphere of Christian giving. This does not mean that the Christian should give less than the tithe. It does mean, however, that it is not law-giving, but love-giving. It is not commandment-giving, but grace-giving. We give, not to keep a law, but to prove our love. We give, not because we are compelled, but because we are impelled. It is an inward impulse and not an outward compulsion.

B. *Example in Giving* (verse 9b)

. . . that, though he was rich, yet for your sakes he became poor, that ye through his poverty might be rich.

Paul referred to Christ as the believer's supreme example in giving. Being rich, He voluntarily became poor that we might be enriched through His poverty.

Christ was rich in power, yet in order to enrich us He voluntarily surrendered this power and became obedient to His Father's will. He was rich in glory, yet in order to enrich us He voluntarily laid aside this glory and assumed the flesh of man. He was rich in honor, yet in order to enrich us He voluntarily surrendered the honors of heaven for the shame of earth. He was rich in wisdom, yet in order to enrich us He voluntarily surrendered the independent use of this wisdom and became subject to His Father's judgment.

With what kind of riches are we enriched? Not, of course, with the riches of gold. Not all that glitters is gold nor is all wealth riches. There are the riches of peace, the riches of a good name, the riches of a clean conscience, the riches of a pure character and the riches of hope. All these are to be found in the riches of God's grace. If you have these riches, you are rich indeed. You then have riches that neither adversity, depression, bankruptcy, ill health or death can take away from you.

A newspaperman once asked Thomas Edison this question: "Mr. Edison, what is electricity?" "I do not know," Edison answered. "I only understand some of the things it will do." "But how do you explain it?" the reporter inquired. "I can't explain it. It just seems to me God has given it to the world to demonstrate His power. I simply take it on faith and go on working."

All that we have in this world is God's gift which we must take on faith and translate into usefulness. Faith takes force and makes it work for us. Salvation is not different from electricity. Electricity is God's power for physical light. Salvation is God's mercy for spiritual light. Neither can be explained. Both must be taken on faith and that faith will translate them into light and power in our lives.

Each of us have certain abilities. Some have the ability to speak and others to sing. All have a certain ability to translate brains and brawn into money. Money becomes a potential power for good or evil. In our hands money is power. It can be used for elevating or debasing purposes. The Bible teaches us its right use. It gives us objectives and incentives for the use of our means. We shall be held accountable for the use of our means as much as for the use of our time and talent.

C. *Pledging in Giving* (verses 10-11)

And herein I give my advice: for this is expedient for you, who have begun before, not only to do, but also to be forward a year ago. Now therefore perform the doing of it; that as there was a readiness to will, so there may be a performance also out of that which ye have.

The Corinthians had made a pledge twelve months before to assist the Judean Christians in their distress. Something had happened to defer their good intentions. Perhaps it was the quarrels and dissensions that had occurred in the church. If so, it is another example of the wasted time and effort of strife. It robs us of our good intentions. It steals our zeal and turns it into channels of bitterness. It causes suffering in those who should be helped by our service.

Paul now urged them to carry out their original purpose and to act promptly in responding to the need of their Christian brethren.

We notice these people had made a pledge to help their brethren in Jerusalem. We often hear of people who say they do not believe in pledging. This is undoubtedly an earnest conviction and yet it is not necessarily a reasonable deduction. The reason usually given is that they do not wish to risk the possibility of failure. Untoward circumstances may hinder. Illness or unemployment or failing investments may occur.

All of us risk these things in everyday life. We turn on our electric lights on the basis of a pledge to pay for them at the end of the month. We use our telephone on the basis of a pledge. We use every utility we have on the basis of a pledge and think nothing about it. And yet in God's work we dare not risk a pledge. Do you not think that God makes allowances for sickness and circumstances beyond our control? Are we to think of Him as an unbending creditor who will hold us to a pledge we cannot keep? How strange it would be were that true. All God asks is a performance in keeping with our ability. It may not be all we intended to do, but it can be all we are able to do.

D. *Willingness in Giving* (verse 12)

For if there be first a willing mind, it is accepted according to that a man hath, and not according to that he hath not.

The test of generosity or faithfulness in our giving is not wealth, but willingness, for "it is accepted according to that a man hath, and not according to that he hath not." This means that if you gave a dollar and someone else gave a hundred dollars that the smallness of your gift would not be measured by the largeness of

the other's gift. The measurement would be according
to what you have and the willingness with which you
gave what you had.

This brings up the matter of giving what we have when
we have it. There are uncounted millions of dollars in
the hands of Christian men and women which are being
held for the day of death to be distributed by the provisions of wills. The wisdom and rightness of this kind
of stewardship is open for question. Naturally we
should be protected against want, but when far more
than enough for our needs is kept in idleness, then it is
wrong.

Someone has said that those who defer their gifts to
their deathbed do as good as say, "Lord, I will give Thee
something when I can keep it no longer." Happy is the
man who is his own executor.

It is even suggested that posthumous giving through
wills, estates and trust funds is outside of the realm of
recognized and rewarded stewardship. We shall be
recognized and rewarded for the "things done in [the]
body" but posthumous giving is done after we have left
the body. Whether this is so is debatable, but it is worthy
of our earnest thought.

We may be sure if Christian stewards will seek the
will of God for the wise use of their means, while they
are alive to execute their own estates, they will find
ample avenues for doing untold good. Think of the
satisfaction derived from seeing one's means transformed into human help and happiness. Consider the
joy of seeing money invested in Gospel enterprise transferred into immortality by the salvation which Christ
brings. A vision of this kind would change our whole
conception of Christian stewardship.

E. *Equality in Giving* (verses 13-15)

For I mean not that other men be eased, and ye burdened: but by
an equality, that now at this time your abundance may be a supply

for their want, that their abundance also may be a supply for your want: that there may be equality: as it is written, He that had gathered much had nothing over; and he that had gathered little had no lack.

The responsibility involved in giving was to be on the basis of equality. This equality was to be judged by ability. As far as the Corinthians were concerned they were then well able to relieve the Judeans. Some day the circumstances might be reversed and the Judeans would be called upon to supply the lack of the Corinthians.

This is not for Corinth only. It is for us as well. The fortunes of life change very quickly. Today we are in abundance and tomorrow we may be in want. Today it is luxury and tomorrow it may be lack. Today we are giving and tomorrow we may be receiving.

The rich are not to be expected to bear all the load and the poor are not to be excused from proportionate responsibility.

To illustrate his point, Paul cited the case of an Israelite who went out to gather manna. He was thrilled with its abundance and being overcome with greed he got together all the pots and jars he could find and filled them with manna. It was far more than he needed or could possibly use but it would not keep and the next morning he found it to be a foul mass of pollution.

In our gathering of the good things of life, let us not forget the greedy Israelite. We can use just so much of this world's substance; beyond that personal use, its hoarding will be a corruption and a curse. Use the surplus for the good of man and the glory of God. It is the surplus of substance that constitutes one of our great problems. Be a diligent and wise gatherer, but also be a generous and wise distributor.

Obligation and opportunity go side by side. For every obligation there is an opportunity of performance.

The Bible speaks of opportunities as doors. It says,

"Behold, I have set before thee an open door." It is the open door of Gospel opportunity and the privilege of service.

"An income," someone has remarked, "is something difficult to live within, and impossible to live without." There are other complications in this matter of income. Either it is too eagerly retained for utterly selfish purposes, or it is too easily used for equally selfish purposes.

What we have earned by toil, should not be dispensed with folly. How we use it is as important as how we acquired it and what we have. We can destroy the value and usefulness of our gifts by unwise stewardship. Therefore, it is to our interest to understand that what we have given is to be properly administered. This was Paul's anxious concern regarding the offering being received at Corinth for Judea.

III. CHRISTIAN CHARITY THROUGH EFFICIENT ADMINISTRATION (verses 16-24)

This phase of Christian giving is dealt with in three ways.

A. *Giving and Using* (verses 16-20)

But thanks be to God, which put the same earnest care into the heart of Titus for you. For indeed he accepted the exhortation; but being more forward, of his own accord he went unto you. And we have sent with him the brother, whose praise is in the gospel throughout all the churches; and not that only, but who was also chosen of the churches to travel with us with this grace, which is administered by us to the glory of the same Lord, and declaration of your ready mind: avoiding this, that no man should blame us in this abundance which is administered by us.

Having asked for the gifts of the Corinthians, Paul now took measures to protect both the gathering and the using of those gifts. The measures he prescribed were not an elaborate system of red tape. The safety of the measures employed was guaranteed by the men used in the gathering and administering. After all, no method is better than the men who administer it. Paul promptly promised the security of their gifts by naming trusted Christian men who would be used by him in his proposed plan to help the Christians at Jerusalem.

The coming of these men, of whom Paul's intimate friend Titus was the leader, was more than a financial mission. Titus was coming to look after the spiritual interests of the Corinthians just as much as the material interests of the Judeans. It says in verse 16, "But thanks be to God, which put the same earnest care into the heart of Titus for you." Titus' care was for the Corinthians. He was not only interested in seeing to the proper handling of the funds, but was exceedingly zealous to see that the Corinthians did not fail to understand the great opportunity that was theirs. If they failed to see it, they would rob themselves of a great blessing.

This tells us that giving is more than extending our hand to bestow a gift. It is expanding our heart to receive grace. Giving makes room. It creates space. It expands the affections so as to enlarge the capacity of our lives for enjoyment. In this light, we understand that whoever gives, blesses himself as well as others.

One of the principal reasons for Paul's careful administration of these relief funds is declared in the 20th verse, "Avoiding this, that no man should blame us in this abundance which is administered by us." It was a preventive against misunderstanding. Paul wished to avoid blame for inefficiency. He sought to preclude possibility of charges of dishonesty.

Of course, no Christ-minded person would have the shadow of a suspicion about Paul's honesty, but there were many who had a ready mind to impugn an honest Christian's motives. Not even Paul's pure purposes and upright life were free from suspicion and slander. "His enemies were contemptible enough to intimate that his interest in the collection was not unselfish and that there was something suspicious about his zeal for the gathering of such large sums." This helps us to understand why Paul insisted on such proper precautions in handling Christian funds.

B. *Giving and Procuring* (verses 21-23)

Providing for honest things, not only in the sight of the Lord, but also in the sight of men. And we have sent with them our brother, whom we have oftentimes proved diligent in many things, but now much more diligent, upon the great confidence which I have in you. Whether any do enquire of Titus, he is my partner and fellow-helper concerning you: or our brethren be enquired of, they are the messengers of the churches, and the glory of Christ.

What Paul expressed in the 21st verse is the ideal of Christian conduct. It says, "Providing for honest things, not only in the sight of the Lord, but also in the sight of men." His activity was henceforth to be judged by honorableness in the sight of both God and man.

Naturally there would be, as we have already seen, a misjudging of the purest motives. Regardless of this, Paul determined that he was going to be careful of his good name and would appear honorable in all things.

This is a worthy purpose. In Christian work, more than in any other, it ought to be true but is often woefully lacking. Its lack is not necessarily an evidence of dishonesty but is cause for criticism. Let us be careful to safeguard ourselves in such a way that honor is always reflected on the cause we serve.

The men whom Paul chose were beyond reproach, so much so that Paul could unhesitatingly say, "They are . . . the glory of Christ." That was a beautiful tribute. These men were an honor to the cause they served. They brought glory to the Christ they followed. Do we? Dare we be brave enough to inquire of ourselves whether we are a credit or a discredit, a glory or a shame to the Master whose name we bear?

C. *Giving and Loving* (verse 24)

Wherefore shew ye to them, and before the churches, the proof of your love, and of our boasting on your behalf.

The meaning here is plain. The proof of love is in giving. The proof of loving God is not in praying. Praying may be one of the most selfish engagements we keep. It can become a religious "give-me" exercise. The proof of loving God is not in worship. Worship may be for the sake of religious respectability. The proof of loving God is in giving one's self to God.

It is so with loving man. Love is peculiarly expressed by our gifts. The first act of love is giving what you are to another in love's troth. The next and continuing act of love is giving what you have.

Love thrives on giving and dies in withholding. Love shrivels and atrophies when confined.

The greatest example of love we have is in God. He "so loved the world, that he gave." Divine love was proved by the divine gift. We are no exception to the rule. Our love will be proved by our gifts.

The thing to do is not to talk about it, but prove it. Look about you. Do your eyes meet the appeal of someone's need? Do not content yourself by saying, "I would if I could." Say, "I will do what I can." Let affection respond to affliction. Only by the practical display of it can we prove the actual possession of it.

The Scripture addresses this pointed question to us, "Whoso hath this world's good, and seeth his brother have need, and shutteth up his bowels of compassion from him, how dwelleth the love of God in him?" The proof of its possession is love in action.

9

THE CHRISTIAN'S PRINCIPLE OF GIVING

2 Corinthians 9

One of the chief causes of the lack of consistent Christian giving is the great dearth of teaching on this New Testament subject. There is a very definite body of teaching to be found and it should be brought to the attention of the Church. The Christian pattern of giving is not to be found in the Old Testament for the authority of the Christian life is a New Testament authority.

With this in mind, let us examine the contents of this chapter where we discover five principles of giving.

  I. THE PRINCIPLE OF READINESS (verses 1-5)
 II. THE PRINCIPLE OF THE HARVEST (verse 6)
III. THE PRINCIPLE OF FREE-WILL (verse 7)
 IV. THE PRINCIPLE OF DIVINE GRACE (verses 8-10)
  V. THE PRINCIPLE OF THANKSGIVING (verses 11-15)

I. THE PRINCIPLE OF READINESS (verses 1-5)

For as touching the ministering to the saints, it is superfluous for me to write to you: for I know the forwardness of your mind, for which I boast of you to them of Macedonia, that Achaia was ready a year ago; and your zeal hath provoked very many. Yet have I sent the brethren, lest our boasting of you should be in vain in this behalf; that, as I said, ye may be ready: lest haply if they of Macedonia come with me, and find you unprepared, we (that we say not, ye) should be ashamed in this same confident boasting. Therefore I thought it necessary to exhort the brethren, that they would go before unto you, and make up beforehand your bounty, whereof ye had notice before, that the same might be ready, as a matter of bounty, and not as of covetousness.

Paul had certain things at stake in regard to this proposed relief offering for the Judeans from the Corinthians.

His pride in the Corinthians was at stake. He had boasted in Macedonia of the liberality and readiness of the Corinthians. What a calamity it would have been if they had not justified his hopes and claims and had been found unwilling and unready to respond to the plight of their fellow Christians. To avoid this, Paul had sent Titus and his companions on ahead to gather the offering beforehand so that when Paul and any of the Macedonians arrived he would not be embarrassed by their possible delinquency.

It was for this reason that he wrote, "Therefore I thought it necessary to exhort the brethren, that they would go before unto you, and make up beforehand your bounty, whereof ye had notice before, that the same might be ready, as a matter of bounty, and not as of covetousness" (verse 5).

The point of interest here is the practical human measures which Paul used to insure the success of his mission. He employed both faith and works. He trusted God and used means. There are extraordinary occasions where divine help is the only hope we have, but I am quite sure God does not intend our faith to be a substitute for our works. Faith is the cause and works are the effect. It seems to be a co-operative engagement and effort. What is evangelism but God's Word sounded forth by human means? This follows through all the enterprises of Christian work and experience.

Paul undoubtedly had great faith in the success of his financial mission in raising funds in Corinth for the Christians at Jerusalem, but he had only asked God to provide these funds and he asked the Corinthians to give them. Furthermore, he not only asked the Corinthians to give, but he organized a financial mission of

three trusted Christian men to go beforehand as a pre-
cautionary measure to take such steps as were necessary
to gather the money.

All of this was both legitimate and proper. It was
that desirable combination of God and man, the divine
and the human, faith and works, trust and action. It
was the balancing of God's power and the human instrument. We fail in not understanding that God works
through the human instrument and not apart from it.

In employing the measures he did, Paul was very
careful to have the Corinthians understand that it was
not to be by coercion, but by co-operation. This was what
he meant by the latter part of the fifth verse, ''That the
same might be ready, as a matter of bounty, and not as
of covetousness.'' Paul sought these funds as an expression of Corinthian generosity and grace and not as
something extorted from them.

The length to which we hear modern ministers go in
taking offerings is often a disgrace to the dignity of
stewardship. They ask people to give large collections
in order to save their reputations for raising money.
Besides this there are appeals of the auctioneer type,
appeals by psychological tricks, appeals to carnal vanity
so that Christianity is demeaned and disgraced.

If these Corinthians were to give on the principle of
readiness, if they were to be ready to meet the need of
others, they must be sensitive to that need. They could
not be sensitive to the need unless they were sympathetic
to their fellow Christians.

It is so easy to become calloused by the frequency and
the commonness of human tragedy. It is so easy to become wrapped up in the comfortable garments of our
own circumstances and to build around ourselves and our
domiciles the high wall of selfish indifference.

This is the surest way there is to become small and
unhappy. Cultivate sympathy and carry a sensitive

spirit and you will find your life flowing into channels of usefulness and happiness. There is a homely phrase "it is better to slop than to skimp." A skimping selfishness reveals a shriveled soul. A withholding hand reveals a withered heart.

II. THE PRINCIPLE OF THE HARVEST (verse 6)

But this I say, He which soweth sparingly shall reap also sparingly; and he which soweth bountifully shall reap also bountifully.

We are too prone to think of giving in terms of duty rather than in terms of bounty. We consider it as an expenditure in charity rather than an investment in life. The fact is, we enrich ourselves when we distribute to others. We read in Proverbs, "He that hath pity upon the poor lendeth unto the Lord; and that which he hath given will he pay him again" (19:17).

The laws of nature operate in the life of the Christian as is illustrated by this law of the harvest. It is the picture of a farmer sowing his spring crop. What he sows in the spring he will harvest in the fall. It is inviolately true that he will reap as he sows. The proportion of his reaping will be determined by the proportion of his sowing. If he sows a few seeds, he will reap a scant harvest, but if he sows generously, he will reap bountifully.

By reason of this law of the harvest, we understand that Christian giving is not a scattering. It is a sowing. It is not a contribution. It is an investment. It is not promiscuous and pointless religious aims. It is an act regulated and rewarded by the law of the harvest transposed into the spiritual realm of Christian experience.

This constitutes a challenge to our faith. Upon the face of it we consider it to be a reasonable expectation. If God's laws in nature protect and prosper the wise farmer, then God's laws in the spiritual realm would be expected to protect and prosper the wise Christian steward.

On the other hand, we may be quite sure this is not intended to materialize and commercialize our giving. The virtue of giving is more than in the gift. It is in the spirit and motive behind the gift. The by-product of genuine Christian giving is this blessing of reaping. Our reaping will be a return in both kind and proportion to our sowing.

The Bible teaches us the enjoyment of giving. It attaches to giving the feeling and exhilaration of enjoyment and pleasure.

III. THE PRINCIPLE OF FREE-WILL (verse 7)

Every man according as he purposeth in his heart, so let him give; not grudgingly, or of necessity: for God loveth a cheerful giver.

Two statements are made here about our giving.

A. *According to Our Purpose*—"Every man according as he purposeth in his heart, so let him give."

This means free-will giving. It means giving without compulsion. In fact, it means giving without regulation or constraint or force of any kind. It is giving by one's own individual intention. It is something free from assessment. The amount of our gift cannot be assigned to us by another. It is solely our choice.

What is to determine our choice, as to the amount of our gift? Are we free to say that we will give a dollar when we are able to give ten? The proportion of the Christian's benevolences is subject to the need and also subject to the Lord. The law of the tenth is a wise and fair proportion, but even this is not the final standard. The higher standard is the Holy Spirit whose promptings will give sensitive Christian souls the most accurate measurement of choice. But, remember, it is to be our choice and by our free-will.

B.   *According to Our Pleasure*—"not grudgingly, or of necessity: for God loveth a cheerful giver."

Instead of giving because of the compulsion of circumstances and custom, we should give because it is our pleasure. It says here that God "loveth a cheerful giver." This means a "hilarious giver."

From this we gather that God's approval and our profit is not to be determined by the amount of our gift, but rather by the spirit in and the motive behind the gift. This is so because in giving God is seeking to develop and enlarge the resources of the giver. Giving is not merely a means of distributing charity. It is a means of developing character. For this reason, God seeks our co-operation in the spirit of joy and love, rather than from compulsion and constraint.

In the last analysis it is a question of Christ's Lordship and our loyalty.

IV. THE PRINCIPLE OF DIVINE GRACE (verses 8-10)

And God is able to make all grace abound toward you; that ye, always having all sufficiency in all things, may abound to every good work (as it is written, He hath dispersed abroad; he hath given to the poor: his righteousness remaineth for ever. Now he that ministereth seed to the sower both minister bread for your food, and multiply your seed sown, and increase the fruits of your righteousness.)

The purpose of divine grace is to increase the resources of the hilarious giver so that he may be able to respond in other cases of need. God's gifts to us are not intended for selfish consumption. They are intended to serve others.

The gift of song is given that it may pour through our lips to others. The gift of writing is given that we may enlighten others. Equally so, the gift of means. Our money is to lighten the load of others. It is intended to be a grace of life used for the blessing of those in need. God gives that we may give. We possess that we may pass on.

There is a great challenge in this principle of giving. Whoever will dare to step out upon this promise of divine grace will have a sufficiency for another's deficiency; he will have an abundance for another's lack.

It says here that "God is able to make all grace abound." The problem is not on the divine side, but the human. With God there is a sufficient ability. He waits only for enterprising children who will dare to believe and act upon this challenging promise. Our sufficiency will be through His supply. This means that by the law of faith we will tap the resources of God and turn them into practical good.

The force of this verse is very intriguing. It is tremendous. It opens a whole new area of possibility. It boldly declares that we may have ample means with which it will be possible to contribute to every good cause. Why are we so poor? Why are we so loath to launch out upon the career of benevolence when we have the unlimited backing of Almighty God?

This is neither fantastic nor foolish. It is factual. It is based upon God's laws of the spiritual world. It shows us that a right attitude plus noble action will put us in the place of power. Let us take the right attitude toward God and toward life, and God will make it possible for us to meet the challenge of great things.

The only reason we do not have "all sufficiency" for all emergencies is because we do not believe it is possible. It is easy for us to say the words in this verse, but it is another thing to put our lives into the place of their power.

V. The Principle of Thanksgiving (verses 11-15)

Being enriched in every thing to all bountifulness, which causeth through us thanksgiving to God. For the administration of this service not only supplieth the want of the saints, but is abundant also by many thanksgivings unto God; whiles by the experiment of this ministration they glorify God for your professed subjection unto the gospel of Christ, and for your liberal distribution unto them, and unto all men; and by their prayer for you, which long after you for the exceeding grace of God in you. Thanks be unto God for his unspeakable gift.

The fitting conclusion of this chapter on giving is this word about thanksgiving. Giving and gratitude are a proper cause and effect. Our gift should awaken gratitude in the receiver's heart.

First, it is gratitude to the human giver that the needs of the saints have been supplied. Wherever this thoughtful remembrance is lacking, the true sense of gratitude is missing. Let us be sure to be thankful. Never let our appreciation be taken for granted.

Second, it is gratitude to the Divine Giver who is the original giver and whose bounty makes it possible to supply others.

Finally, it is gratitude to God for His "unspeakable gift" which no doubt refers to the source and inspiration of all Christian benevolence—Jesus Christ. Christ is the gift of God and the source of all Christian grace and benevolence.

Section III

THE COMMENDATIONS OF THE CHRISTIAN

2 Corinthians 10—13

10

THE COMMENDATION OF CHRIST

2 Corinthians 10

The final section of this book deals with a matter of vital importance to all Christians. The Christian is the recipient of something, but he is also the giver of something. He has a contribution to make on the basis of what he has received. His contribution is one of life and service.

In this life and service he is to be judged by his performance and not by his profession. Nowhere in the Bible is a man justified by what he says about himself. He is judged by certain intrinsic qualities and certain outward activities.

From this point on we have a continuance of Paul's biographical account of himself. It is such an account as will find its application in all Christian thinking and living. It points out to us those things which commend a Christian.

The sense of the chapter is found in the last verse, "For not he that commendeth himself is approved, but whom the Lord commendeth."

I. THE CHRISTIAN'S ATTITUDE (verses 1-6)
II. THE CHRISTIAN'S AUTHORITY (verses 7-11)
III. THE CHRISTIAN'S APPROVAL (verses 12-18)

I. THE CHRISTIAN'S ATTITUDE (verses 1-6)

Now I Paul myself beseech you by the meekness and gentleness of Christ, who in presence am base among you, but being absent am

bold toward you: but I beseech you, that I may not be bold when I
am present with that confidence, wherewith I think to be bold against
some, which think of us as if we walked according to the flesh. For
though we walk in the flesh, we do not war after the flesh: (for the
weapons of our warfare are not carnal, but mighty through God to
the pulling down of strong holds;) casting down imaginations, and
every high thing that exalteth itself against the knowledge of God,
and bringing into captivity every thought to the obedience of Christ;
and having in a readiness to revenge all disobedience, when your
obedience is fulfilled.

The Bible deals in practical things. It deals with the
common things that occur in our ordinary experiences.
It is not a religious book for the cloister but a spiritual
book for the home.

The problem before us is the oft recurring problem
of human relations. It presents itself frequently in our
experience. It is found in the home in the relation of one
family member to another. It is found in the community
in the relation of one neighbor to another. It is found
in the church in the relation of one Christian to another.

The relation of one Christian to another has the possibilities and prospects of the sweetest fellowship on
earth, but if we are not careful it can turn into the bit-
terest experience on earth. Former brethren can become bitter, recriminative and vicious. They can completely forget their Master who exercised the greatest
tolerance and forbearance. When wronged He never
sought vengeance. The injustices against Him were more
useful in furthering His ministry than if all men had
been fair to Him. These things Christians are prone to
forget; they allow carnality the ascendancy and thus
seek to establish their personal cause at the expense of
the Master's. All the time their personal animosities
are being fought, their Master's cause is suffering and
languishing.

Paul found himself the victim of injustice, illtreat-
ment, false report and personal abuse. The circumstances of this attack grew out of Paul's residence and

labors in Corinth. For the space of a year and a half
he had given himself, his time and his energy in prayer
and teaching. Through God's blessing upon his in-
defatigable labors he had seen a little colony of Christians grow in a truly remarkable manner. When the
church reached the stage of maturity where they could
carry on what Paul had commenced, he moved on to
other and larger fields of activity.

Since leaving Corinth Paul had heard of a preconceived effort on the part of certain local enemies to
sabotage his character and reputation. They had succeeded in turning Paul's converts away from confidence
in him. They had succeeded in destroying the friendship of Paul's old friends. What was worse, these
personal enemies were stopping at no lengths to so effectively damage Paul's reputation as a servant of Christ
as to make it difficult for him to carry on his ministry.

What a sad state of affairs this was. How lamentable
that weapons of hatred, animosity and wickedness were
being turned upon this man of God in a diabolical
attempt to hinder his usefulness and service. We can
be grateful for this unpleasant experience in Paul's
life, because the lessons in personal conduct and Christian behavior which it teaches will enable us to meet
situations of a similar nature whenever they arise in
our life.

Paul's experience presents not only a cross-section of
Christian experience, but also the ideals of Christian
behavior. It is for our profit that Paul suffered. It
will be to our credit and ultimate vindication and
triumph if we heed these lessons.

Notice what happened. Paul moved out and other
leaders moved in who were neither of the spiritual
stature or nature of the great apostle. They immediately set about to build up their own reputations by destroying Paul's reputation. They set about to win the

affection of these Corinthians by destroying their affection for Paul. In order to be loved, they insisted on Paul being hated. In order to be liked, they insisted on Paul being disliked. In order to be held in esteem, they insisted on Paul's person and labors being held in contempt.

In their desperate search for a case against Paul with which to carry on their sabotage they could find nothing wrong with his preaching, or his doctrine, or his moral conduct, so they took up purely personal matters. It was a perfect revelation of their own diminutive stature and their own ignoble character. They attacked Paul purely on differences of opinion. They took certain characteristics of Paul and magnified them out of all proportion and sought to use these to destroy him.

The first thing they attacked was Paul's personal appearance. They tried to reflect upon the legitimacy of his apostleship on the grounds of his physical presence.

The closest idea we have of Paul's personal appearance is as follows: "Paul is set before us as having the strongly marked and prominent features of a Jew, yet not without some of the finer lines indicative of Greek thought. His stature was diminutive, and his body disfigured by some lameness or distortion which may have provoked the contemptuous expressions of his enemies. His beard was long and thin. His head was bald. The characteristics of his face were a transparent complexion, which visibly betrayed the quick changes of his feelings, a bright grey eye under thickly overhanging eyebrows, a cheerful and winning expression of countenance which invited the approach and inspired the confidence of strangers. It would be natural to infer, from his continual journeys and manual labor, that he was possessed of great strength of constitution. But men of delicate health have often gone through the greatest exertions, and his own words on more than one occasion show that he suffered much from bodily infirmity.''

How did Paul meet this challenge to his life's usefulness? What he did indicates more than anything else the genuineness of his Christian character. It tells us more than the mighty oratory at the Areopagus. He began his reply with these simple and beautiful words of the first verse, ''Now I Paul myself beseech you by the meekness and gentleness of Christ.'' Weymouth's translation says, ''By the gentleness and reasonableness of Christ.''

Paul's most effective vindication would not come by means of the approval of many, but by following the example of his Master. In this crisis Paul determined to be Christian. He might have employed force or used the authority of his apostleship or established his claims before the tribunal. Instead, he appealed to Christ. If they thought well of Christ, they would look differently at Paul. If they were eager to follow Christ and give a genuine exhibition of Christlikeness, they would withdraw their carnal and childish differences and seek to establish Christ's cause in the world.

Here is a case of practical Christianity. It presents all the possibilities of Christian nobility. It offers the opportunity of rising above the small and petty activities of carnal men and living in the lofty and noble realm of Christlikeness.

Someone has said that ''Christianity as it works in the heart, is mightier than it is when explained and enforced in a thousand volumes. Christianity in books is like seed in the granary, dry and all but dead. It is not written, but living characters, that are to convert the infidel. The lives of good men and not the library of theologues, is the converting power.''

Much, though not all truth, lies in that declaration. While our example does not convert others, it at least attracts them to the Word which does convert them. The alluring sight of a living Christianity has enough arresting power to stop the most morally profligate and the most intellectually sophisticated.

We continue to see Paul in action under abuse and malediction. He did not lose his self-control because he was controlled by Christ. He did not lose his spiritual dignity, nor his equilibrium, nor his awareness of being Christ's servant.

The principles of Paul's life are revealed in this remarkable statement: "For though we walk in the flesh, we do not war after the flesh: (for the weapons of our warfare are not carnal, but mighty through God to the pulling down of strong holds;) casting down imaginations, and every high thing that exalteth itself against the knowledge of God, and bringing into captivity every thought to the obedience of Christ."

Whatever conflict or controversy he was engaged in was fought on this basis. Whatever difficult task he was confronted with was attacked by this means. Whatever service he was to render was done by this method. It is something for us to follow.

None of us is exempt from conflict, difficulty or obligation. We can meet these things either as Christians or as pagans, either as new men or old men, either as spiritually minded or carnally minded, either with the weapons of the flesh or the weapons of the Spirit.

Paul said that he walked in the flesh but did not war after the flesh. He was compelled to walk as a man walks, by sight and sound, to live by brain or brawn and to meet the problems of a world of men and women of flesh. While this was a necessity by force of unchangeable circumstance, Paul did not forget that he belonged to a new race and a new people. He was a Christian and a new creation. He was indwelt by God and united to powers and forces of superhuman capacity and ability.

His strength did not lie in his flesh but in his spirit. His conflict was not to be one of force against force, flesh against flesh, anger against anger, feeling against feeling. His strategy was that of the Spirit. His was not the blitzkrieg of the flesh but the power of faith.

This was so because he did not wrestle "against flesh and blood, but against principalities, against powers, against the rulers of the darkness of this world, against spiritual wickedness in high places." Therefore his weapons of defense and offense were "the whole armour of God." They were truth, righteousness, faith, prayer and the Word of God.

These are the weapons of the Christian's warfare. Let us remember this and go to the arsenal of the soul instead of the place of acrimony and strife.

A. *The Christian's Weapons Are Mighty* (verse 4)

   1.   In Their Contrast

They are not carnal. They are not the weak weapons of the flesh. They are not the puny abilities of sinful man. They are not of this world. Paul was surrounded by all sorts of philosophies and systems of religion. They were weak and impotent to help men. Paul had access to instruments of great power. They were these weapons of the Spirit. With them he could raze mighty strongholds; he could conquer formidable enemies; he could blast away bitter opposition; he could destroy evil influences.

Herein lies potential power for each of us. We have failed to fully appreciate the great power at our disposal. It is to our shame that in times of conflict and difficulty we have turned away from this arsenal of the soul to use the ineffectual weapons of the flesh. It has always been to our sorrow. In the light of past failures, let us turn to our present opportunities with a new determination to use these mighty weapons and instruments of God.

2. In Their Character

Their character is spiritual. Their might is "through God." They connect the Christian with the invisible power of God. They link him with divine energy. They unite him with forces of irresistible might.

3. In Their Conquest

Arthur S. Way's rendering of verse 5 is positively thrilling: "I can batter down bulwarks of human reason, I can scale every crag-fortress that towers up, bidding defiance to the true knowledge of God. I can make each rebel purpose my prisoner-of-war, and bow it into submission to Messiah." *

Yes, these weapons of the soul are mighty in their conquest. Christ's disciples have conquered more by love than by hate, more by faith than by flesh, more by prayer than by propaganda.

England's first day of prayer in the present conflict was followed by what newspaper correspondents and war analysts are calling "The Miracle of Dunkirk." One Arthur Divine writes this:

I am still amazed about the whole Dunkirk affair. There was from first to last, a queer, medieval sense of miracle about it. You remember the old quotation about the miracle that crushed the Spanish Armada, "God sent a wind." This time "God withheld the wind." Had we had one on-shore breeze of any strength at all, in the first days, we would have lost a hundred thousand men.

The pier at Dunkirk was the unceasing target of bombs and shell-fire throughout, yet it never was hit. Two hundred and fifty thousand men embarked from that pier. Had it been blasted . . .

The whole thing from first to last was covered with that same strange feeling of something supernatural. We muddled, we quarreled, everybody swore and was bad-tempered and made the wildest accusations of inefficiency and worse in high places. Boats were badly handled and broke down, arrangements went wrong.

And yet out of all that mess we beat the experts, we defied the law and the prophets, and where the Government and the Board of Admiralty had hoped to bring away 30,000 men, we brought away 335,000. If that was not a miracle, there are no miracles left.

*S. Way, *Letters of Paul, Hebrews, Book of Psalms*. (Kregel Publ.), p. 81.

The greatest spiritual weapon at our command is the Word of God. It is a Book of divine power. It has survived all its enemies. "The empire of Cæsar is gone; the legions of Rome are moldering in the dust; the avalanches that Napoleon hurled upon Europe have melted away; the pride of the Pharaohs has fallen; the pyramids they have raised to be their tombs are sinking every day in the desert sands; Tyre is the rock for bleaching fishermen's nets; Sidon has scarcely left a wreck behind; but the Word of God still survives. All things that threatened to extinguish it have only aided it; and it only proves every day how transient the noblest monument that man can build, how enduring is the least word God has spoken. Tradition has dug for it a grave; intolerance has lighted for it many a faggot; many a Judas has betrayed it with a kiss; many a Demas has forsaken it, but the Word of God still endures."

Complications frequently arise which require our judgment and decision. We must judge between the counterfeit and the genuine. Everything genuine has its counterfeit. It seems as though almost all things exist in doubles; not duplicates but doubles. One is the substance and the other is the shadow. There is the saint and the hypocrite, the doctor and the quack, the merchant and the faker, the statesman and the demagogue, the philosopher and the charlatan. So it is that truth and error, illumination and illusion are to be found throughout our life. Our judgment and decision is required in these things.

We must also judge between the false and true criticisms of Christian brethren. Bitter criticisms and condemnations were being made of Paul. He was replying to these not to judge or to engage in carnal controversy but to further his influence as a servant of Christ. Such a motive was laudable and proper.

II. THE CHRISTIAN'S AUTHORITY (verses 7-11)

Do ye look on things after the outward appearance? If any man trust to himself that he is Christ's, let him of himself think this again, that, as he is Christ's, even so are we Christ's. For though I should boast somewhat more of our authority, which the Lord hath given us for edification, and not for your destruction, I should not be ashamed: that I may not seem as if I would terrify you by letters. For his letters, say they, are weighty and powerful; but his bodily presence is weak, and his speech contemptible. Let such an one think this, that, such as we are in word by letters when we are absent, such will we be also in deed when we are present.

The criticism against Paul was not against his character or his career as a minister of Christ. They found nothing wrong with the efficiency of his ministry or his personal conduct. They were descending to petty assertions about Paul's person and presence.

The word "Paul" means "little one" and they played up this physical characteristic by saying that "his bodily presence is weak, and his speech contemptible." Besides this, they said that when he was away his letters were severe and vigorous and overbearing. In other words, they charged Paul with being brave from a distance and cowardly in person.

It is a good thing to know what one's critics say, for in this way we may discover weaknesses in ourselves that our own judgment does not see. Someone has called his critics the unpaid sentinels of his soul. Another has said, "Men know not themselves by themselves alone." May grace bring us then to the place where we shall be thankful for the criticism as well as the commendation.

Of course there is harmful as well as helpful criticism. If we are in this way to wash one another's feet, we must be careful that the water is not too hot. Bitter criticism of another's actions may proceed from ignorance of his motives. Criticism may scald rather than cleanse.

None of us is beyond the place of improvement.

Knowing this we should seek that state of growth in grace where we may profit and learn by the adversities, injustices and criticisms that come our way.

Paul answered his critics by challenging the method of their criticism. He said, "Do ye look on things after the outward appearance?" They were judging by appearance—by eye value. It was a poor and inaccurate way to judge. No one can properly judge another in this way. Those who claimed prior excellence over Paul because of physical characteristics were no better than Paul in actuality.

Paul enjoyed, as every Christian does, the authority of equality in Christ. He said, "As he is Christ's, even so are we Christ's." That is, one person is no better than another just because he looks better or has more. There is an equality of birth—this time the new birth. There is an equality of place—this time our place in Christ. Disciples are not to be judged by appearances, but by the character.

This should come as a great encouragement to those who have retired in too much modesty when they felt their own inferiority of place and possession. After all, usefulness is not on the basis of who we are, but upon the basis of whose we are. We are Christ's, and in Christ there is the power and ability and privilege of a great usefulness. Let no one displace or discourage us from that usefulness by judging us on appearances. We must recognize the great prerogatives that are our Christian birthright and act upon them.

III. The Christian's Approval (verses 12-18)

For we dare not make ourselves of the number, or compare ourselves with some that commend themselves: but they measuring themselves by themselves, and comparing themselves among themselves, are not wise. But we will not boast of things without our measure, but according to the measure of the rule which God hath distributed to us, a measure to reach even unto you. For we stretch not ourselves beyond our measure, as though we reached not unto you: for we are come as far as to you also in preaching the gospel of Christ: not boasting of things without our measure, that is, of other men's labours; but having hope, when your faith is increased, that we shall be enlarged by you according to our rule abundantly, to preach the gospel in the regions beyond you, and not to boast in another man's line of things made ready to our hand. But he that glorieth, let him glory in the Lord. For not he that commendeth himself is approved, but whom the Lord commendeth.

In the final analysis it is not the approval of ourselves which matters. So said Paul in the final verse, "For not he that commendeth himself is approved, but whom the Lord commendeth."

In verse 12 Paul referred to those who were comparing and commending themselves by this self-chosen standard of self-judgment. He said (we use Way's rendering), "I cannot degrade myself by stooping to their level, by comparing my claims with those of some who stand sponsors for themselves: They measure their own worth by a standard of their own: They compare themselves with themselves—fools that they are."

Paul then reviewed his own activities, not in the light of his own self-chosen standards but rather in the light of Christ's standards.

It takes a great deal of candor and courage to judge ourselves apart from our own feelings. We like to appear well to ourselves. When we go on in self-approval we are liable to perpetuate personal liabilities and faults. If we would be brave enough to submit our motives and actions to the scrutiny of Christ and the indwelling Holy Spirit and then consent to whatever correction is necessary, we would find our lives revolutionized. The question is, do we want a revolution or are we content with the status quo?

11

THE COMMENDATION OF SINCERITY
2 Corinthians 11

One of the greatest personal assets in life and life's work is sincerity. None of the other attributes or attainments we may have are of any intrinsic value unless supported by sincerity. An insincere intellectualism is a cultural veneer which degrades the mind. An insincere profession of religion is a sham which is a shame to the cause of Christ.

Paul had become the target of much abuse and evil criticism. Here he has referred to the quality of sincerity to prove that his life has been right.

The chapter divides into two almost equal parts.

I. SINCERITY AND SERVICE (verses 1-15)
II. SINCERITY AND SUFFERING (verses 16-33)

I. SINCERITY AND SERVICE (verses 1-15)

Three things are apparent in connection with the service we render.

A. *The Motives of Service* (verses 1-6)

Would to God ye could bear with me a little in my folly: and indeed bear with me. For I am jealous over you with godly jealousy: for I have espoused you to one husband, that I may present you as a chaste virgin to Christ. But I fear, lest by any means, as the serpent beguiled Eve through his subtilty, so your minds should be corrupted from the simplicity that is in Christ. For if he that cometh preacheth another Jesus, whom we have not preached, or if ye receive another spirit, which ye have not received, or another gospel, which ye have not accepted, ye might well bear with him. For I suppose I was not a whit behind the very chiefest apostles. But though I be rude in speech, yet not in knowledge; but we have been thoroughly made manifest among you in all things.

The things about which the apostle was writing were the subject of scrutiny at Corinth. Certain workers had come to Corinth after Paul left and had set about to discredit Paul and his work. Paul's appeal for their approval of him was the sincerity of his service.

There is a sense in which our justification is twofold. In God's sight, faith justifies. In man's sight, work justifies. In fact the Scriptures say, "faith without works is dead." This is the point at which law and grace are reconciled. The New Testament way of life is not the Old Testament way. We are saved by grace, but when grace saves it produces in its place the fulfillment of the law. This does not mean that the old Mosaic commandments are revived and that we are to be regimented by a system of legalistic obedience. It does mean, however, that the inner law of grace supersedes the outer law of commandments. At the same time the evidence of faith is in works, but it is works inspired by faith. Works are the effect of faith and not the cause of it.

Thus, the only way to show our faith to men, is by our works. God sees the quality of our faith by His own divine knowledge while man sees the reality of our faith by his human observation.

The saving element of faith is in our believing, while the evidential element of faith is in our doing. When Abraham believed God, he was justified in God's sight. But not until Abraham offered Isaac in sacrifice did he prove his faith. Faith is not only a feeling; it is an act.

We must be careful to preserve the distinction between faith and works. We are justified when we believe, but not until we live out that inner justification will men count us as just men. The cause of justification is faith, while the effect of justification is works.

So far as God was concerned, He accepted Paul's service because of its faith, but so far as man was concerned, he accepted Paul's service because of its works. One of the most convincing evidences was the apostle's sincerity. His motives were not personal. He was actually jealous for the spiritual progress of his converts. He had espoused them to Christ and could not be content unless he saw them continuing in blessing and growth.

B. *The Rewards of Service* (verses 7-11)

Have I committed an offence in abasing myself that ye might be exalted, because I have preached to you the gospel of God freely? I robbed other churches, taking wages of them, to do you service. And when I was present with you, and wanted, I was chargeable to no man: for that which was lacking to me the brethren which came from Macedonia supplied: and in all things I have kept myself from being burdensome unto you, and so will I keep myself. As the truth of Christ is in me, no man shall stop me of this boasting in the regions of Achaia. Wherefore? because I love you not? God knoweth.

Paul's sincerity was never in such conspicuous evidence as when it revealed his attitude to remuneration for his service. Of course there were economic requirements which must be met and these were not to be viewed impractically.

Paul referred to his own carefulness in desiring to be chargeable to no man. He even labored with his own hands so as to be economically independent. When it was necessary to have support, he accepted it from other sources so as to preach gratuitously to the Corinthians.

How far should a modern servant of Christ go in expecting support for himself in pursuance of his service? Certainly not as a payment but rather as a means of continuing in service. Christian service is not to be computed by the dollar value. Whatever is received is not to be considered as a wage, but as a support. It is for the sake of creating economic freedom so as to release all the worker's time and talents for his service.

The question of how much is always persistently present. Here it is a matter of circumstances and for the sake of giving freedom for the more important spiritual tasks to which the worker is committed.

C. *The Counterfeits of Service* (verses 12-15)

But what I do, that I will do, that I may cut off occasion from them which desire occasion; that wherein they glory, they may be found even as we. For such are false apostles, deceitful workers, transforming themselves into the apostles of Christ. And no marvel; for Satan himself is transformed into an angel of light. Therefore it is no great thing if his ministers also be transformed as the ministers of righteousness; whose end shall be according to their works.

Here is the shadow counterfeiting the substance and the false imitating the true. There were such in Paul's day and their kind still exist in our day. It is the conduct of a religious masquerade for the purpose of personal advantage.

The presence of these children of darkness among the children of light is not an incredible thing. They have an origin and a sponsor. Their master is Satan who is "transformed into an angel of light."

Knowing these things to be true, we should be watchfully careful. We should be on our guard against their spurious effort. We should discover them and avoid them.

Nothing will prove the sincerity of our purposes like the enduring of suffering. While suffering proves the sincerity of our purpose, it does not necessarily prove that those purposes are right.

Men have suffered untold agonies in order to gain wealth. They have suffered for political and religious causes which have proved false and wrong. One cannot read *Out of the Night* by Jan Valtin without realizing how sincerely men suffer for delusions. For the furtherance of communism this man was willing to make any sacrifice and to endure indescribable sufferings. His sufferings proved his sincerity but they did not make his cause right.

When we look at this page from Paul's life, we gaze

upon a record of unparalleled experience. He had been ridiculed by his enemies and every conceivable effort had been made to discredit him. These nefarious detractors tried to undo Paul's ministry and to destroy his influence by suggesting that he was prompted by selfish and insincere motives. Paul answered these calumniators by reviewing his service, and then disputed their assertions by demonstrating his sincerity through his sufferings.

II. Sincerity and Suffering (verses 16-33)

Before describing the sufferings which prove his sincerity, Paul followed a line of argument which was suggested by his opponents. It is a form of ridicule but such as is genuine and legitimate. His opponents were proud and carnal boasters who were always seeking to elevate themselves above Paul by recounting their own deeds and experiences. Paul turned the ridicule they had heaped upon him back upon them. He used their weapons. If they had things to boast of, so did he. If they had a record to display, so did he. He not only matched them, but exceeded them and justified his claims by his performance.

The claims of Paul's opponents centered around two things.

A. *What They Once Were* (verse 22)

Are they Hebrews? so am I. Are they Israelites? so am I. Are they the seed of Abraham? So am I.

They boasted of a proud lineage. They gloried in their ancestry. Theirs was the aristocracy of birth. They were gloating over their past Jewish relationship. It was first as "Hebrews," then as "Israelites" and finally as "the seed of Abraham." The first was racial. The second was national. The third was religious. They were called Hebrews because they were those who had "crossed over" leaving Chaldea behind and forming the nucleus of a new race. They were Israelites because of Jacob or Israel whose twelve sons became the national structure of their commonwealth. They were the seed of Abraham because herein lay the religious significance of the Jews. It included the promise of a land, a people and a purpose. Their great purpose in the world was a religious or redemptive one. Consequently Judaism came into being and out of it grew Christianity. It is still true that in these people all the families of the earth will be blessed.

Whatever his opponents claimed to be, Paul was. He too was a Hebrew, an Israelite and of the seed of Abraham.

B. *What They Now Are* (verse 23)

Are they ministers of Christ? (I speak as a fool) I am more; in labours more abundant, in stripes above measure, in prisons more frequent, in deaths oft.

Paul's opponents boasted of being servants of Christ. Paul could boast of that and he adds "much more." He cited proof of this, for he had good reasons for making this superior claim. His reasons are his sufferings. They are an evidence of his deep sincerity.

Many times people have become religious or have changed religious belief because of personal advantage and temporal benefit. With Paul it was not a change of religion which he experienced, but a change of heart and life. This change gave him cause for the endurance of his unspeakable sufferings. It gave him the secret of a noble life. It linked him with a source of strength and comfort which enabled him to live triumphantly in the midst of great adversity.

Consider these evidences of Paul's sincerity: "In labours more abundant, in stripes above measure, in prisons more frequent, in deaths oft. Of the Jews five

times received I forty stripes save one. Thrice was
I beaten with rods, once was I stoned, thrice I suffered
shipwreck, a night and a day I have been in the deep;
in journeyings often, in perils of waters, in perils of
robbers, in perils by mine own countrymen, in perils by
the heathen, in perils in the city, in perils in the wilder-
ness, in perils in the sea, in perils among false brethren;
in weariness and painfulness, in watchings often, in
hunger and thirst, in fastings often, in cold and naked-
ness. Besides those things that are without, that which
cometh upon me daily, the care of all the churches. Who
is weak, and I am not weak? who is offended, and I
burn not?'' (Verses 23-29).

What did Paul do about these sufferings? What was
his reaction? Did he say that Christianity exacts too
great a price? Did he lament his lot and say it was too
hard? Did he rebel against God and blame Him for
his adversities? Not at all.

He considered his adversities a privilege. He gloried
instead of complained. He reviewed this long list of
sufferings and said, ''If I must needs glory, I will glory
of the things which concern mine infirmities.''

Here was the essential difference between Paul and
his opponents. They gloried in their triumphs. Paul
gloried in his tragedies. They gloried in their pleasures.
Paul gloried in his pain. They gloried in their opportunities. Paul gloried in his infirmities. They gloried
in the things that made them strong. Paul gloried
in his weaknesses. They gloried in outward appearances, in popularity and applause. Paul gloried in the
treasures of the soul, in honesty, sincerity and the
approval of God.

We are troubled with the problem of suffering without considering the purpose of suffering. The problem
has no solution except we understand its purpose.

We prune our trees in order to improve them and to

induce growth and fruit. If you wish a tree to grow on a certain side, you prune it there. Then, where one blossom came previously, two more will appear. Fruit will be abundant when pain has been apparent.

Much of the benefit of seemingly adverse experiences results from our attitude. If Paul's attitude had been less than it was, his blessing would not have been as much as it was. If he had complained instead of gloried, he would have felt the complainer's woe and grief. Instead, he took the utility attitude. Whether it was shipwreck, beating, prison, robbers or weariness, it was to be for his ultimate good.

While Paul suffered, he was not overwhelmed. He came out at last as victor rather than victim. This cannot be said of Paul's enemies and the early tyrants and persecutors of Christianity. Those who sought to destroy these Christians came themselves to destruction. And what destruction it was!

Nero was driven from his throne and, perceiving his life in danger, became his own executioner; Domitian was killed by his own servants; Hadrian died of a distressing disease, which was accompanied by great mental agony; Severus never prospered in his affairs after he persecuted the Church, and was killed by the treachery of his son; Maximinus reigned but three years, and died a violent death; Decius was drowned in a marsh, and his body never found; Valerian was taken prisoner by the Persians, and after enduring the horrors of captivity for several years, was flayed alive; Diocletian was compelled to resign his empire, and became insane; Maximanus Valerius was deprived of his government, and strangled himself; Maximanus Galerius was suddenly and awfully removed by death.

12

THE COMMENDATION OF EXPERIENCE

2 Corinthians 12

Men lay great stress on experience. It is considered an important recommendation for employment. When our experience is of the right sort, it provides us commendation and gives us access to man's favor.

Since we are dealing with the biographical record of a distinguished Christian's career, we find his rich and varied experiences a source of approving commendation.

The experiences related in this chapter are of a threefold nature.

   I. THE EXPERIENCE OF PRIVILEGE (verses 1-6)
  II. THE EXPERIENCE OF PAIN (verses 7-10)
 III. THE EXPERIENCE OF PRACTICE (verses 11-21)

I. THE EXPERIENCE OF PRIVILEGE (verses 1-6)

It is not expedient for me doubtless to glory. I will come to visions and revelations of the Lord. I knew a man in Christ above fourteen years ago, (whether in the body, I cannot tell; or whether out of the body, I cannot tell: God knoweth;) such an one caught up to the third heaven. And I knew such a man, (whether in the body, or out of the body, I cannot tell: God knoweth;) how that he was caught up into paradise, and heard unspeakable words, which it is not lawful for a man to utter. Of such an one will I glory: yet of myself I will not glory, but in mine infirmities. For though I would desire to glory, I shall not be a fool; for I will say the truth: but now I forbear, lest any man should think of me above that which he seeth me to be, or that he heareth of me.

This was a remarkable and unusual experience. We shall see that it was the personal experience of Paul.

If there were any occasion to boast and glory, Paul

was determined to relate such things as would prove the reality of his Christian experience. He was not an impostor. He was not a place-seeker nor an opportunist. How unlike his opponents he proved to be was shown in his previous statement, "If I must needs glory, I will glory of the things which concern mine infirmities." These were tangible and common things. They were related to the usual run of life. But, there were uncommon, unusual and outstanding happenings in Paul's experience.

It was such an experience that Paul now related to prove his relationship to God. It was such an experience of which one scarcely dares speak and when Paul did, he spoke of it as though it had happened in the life of another. He humbly and timidly drew the veil aside to reveal one of the most sacred moments of his whole life.

It was an experience with what we call the occult world. However, it is far from the so-called occult experiences of our day. In our day the occult stands for spiritism, astrology and other arts of divination. It is a system of unscientific and unscriptural speculation.

Paul's experience with the unseen world was genuinely occult. As we examine it, we will find it free of any of the instruments that occultists say are necessary for communication with this unseen world. He did not use the services of a medium. He did not employ darkness and there was none of the hypnosis that is used by professional occultists. In fact, Paul did not seek the experience at all. It came unexpectedly and as the result of a murderous assault upon him.

In the first place, you will notice it was a genuinely Christian experience. Paul said, "I knew a man in Christ." The man who had this occult experience was qualified for it by the new birth. He had a spiritual

life. He was identified with God. He was in touch with
the supreme source of life and light in the unseen world.

This is the first requirement of such an experience.
The new birth, and not the natural birth, is necessary.
Flesh and blood cannot inherit nor inhabit nor communi-
cate with the kingdom of heaven. The only source of
communication is the spiritual.

The occultism of our day is proof of an unseen world,
but it is such a world as Paul described in Ephesians
6:12 where he spoke of it in terms of ''the darkness of
this world'' and ''spiritual wickedness in high places.''
There is indeed an occult world which unregenerate men
contact, but it is a Satan-dominated world. It is a world
of darkness and spiritual wickedness.

Paul's experience had no connection with this occult
world of Satan. His was the experience of ''a man in
Christ.'' He touched the unseen world where the living
Christ is present. It is a world of light and beauty.

No informed or rational person will deny that there
is another world just beyond the reach of our senses.
This branch of real occult science has never been
developed. The possibility of telepathic communication
is just beyond us. The limitations of flesh prevent us
from reaching this world of spiritual wonder. However,
some day, when death releases us from this physical
vehicle, we shall enter this world of wonder. Until that
time comes we must content ourselves with very meager
information such as Paul provided in the recital of his
experience.

Paul said the experience he had was fourteen years
previous: ''I knew a man in Christ above fourteen
years ago.'' When we go back into the calendar of
events in Paul's life, we find that fourteen years prior
to the time he was writing this second letter to Corinth,
he was on a preaching tour which included such cities
of Galatia as Antioch, Iconium, Derbe and Lystra.

While at Lystra it is recorded that "there came thither
certain Jews from Antioch and Iconium, who persuaded
the people, and, having stoned Paul, drew him out of the
city, supposing he had been dead" (Acts 14:19). There
they left him, to all intents and purposes, a dead man.
The sequel is this, "Howbeit, as the disciples stood round
about him, he rose up, and came into the city."

This was the time and circumstance of the experience
now being related about "a man in Christ" who was
"caught up to the third heaven." The body of Paul
was outside the city of Lystra, but the person which was
Paul was "caught up." We read that he was caught up
"to the third heaven." The first heaven is our atmos-
pheric heaven; beyond that is the sidereal or starry
heavens; and beyond that sphere of the stars and planets
is another world of spiritual wonder where Christ is. It
is that unseen world which is as real as our seen world.
There the vehicle of the spirit is a spiritual body. Here
the vehicle of the soul is a physical body. They are not
the same worlds, but they are both real and tangible.

Paul described this world as "paradise." The word
"paradise" is found only three times in the New Testament. It is a Persian word written in Greek, meaning "a
royal garden."

Jesus used this word when speaking to the thief on
the cross who begged for remembrance when Christ
came into His kingdom. This made the kingdom and
paradise one and the same place. It is a descriptive
reference to the unseen world beyond our physical sphere
—an unseen world which is the abode of those who have
gone on in death.

Therefore, it is interesting to notice that it is called
a garden. It must be a place of beauty. It must also be
a place of material reality. To us, the great beyond may
be occult or hidden, but to those who are there, it must
be a place of substance and reality.

It is not speculation to conclude that we are to inhabit spheres and worlds in this vast universe which are yet unknown to us. If we inhabit a planet called the earth now, is it incredible that we should inhabit another sphere somewhere else? Of course, in the final phase, the Bible describes the renovation of our present planet for the inhabitation of God's children. However, we are not amiss in thinking that the unseen sphere called paradise is a place of material reality. The spirit is just as real as the body. The body has cellular substance that has size and shape. The spiritual body will have another kind of substance suited to the new kind of life that is to be found beyond the veil of sense.

Most of us think about the other world in terms of ghostly vagueness, as if it were some kind of haven for mysterious spirits that flit and vanish in the air.

We have every Scriptural and reasonable right to believe it to be a world as tangible and as real as ours. In fact, it will be more so, for it will be a world liberated from the liabilities of this present one. It will be perfect and complete and in it we shall exist with the maximum contentment and joy.

If we were to attempt to explain the reason for the present debacle of civilization, many ideas would be expressed. Of course, any explanation would include more than one cause. There would be the common items of greed, dishonesty, politics and irreligion. These are not all. There are ramifications to our plight that few suspect. If we delved deeply enough, we would uncover a major contributing cause. It is our loss of faith in the reality of immortality. By immortality we do not mean what is commonly meant, but that indisputable fact that life never dies—the fact that each of us and all of us, regardless of our paganism or Christianity, our faith or our unbelief, our good or our evil, will live in a state of life beyond death. Somewhere and sometime, we shall be answerable to a Supreme Being whom the Bible reveals as God.

The collapse of our phase of civilization has been caused by materialism. Dictators ran amuck in the world because, for them, God does not exist. If they believed themselves answerable for their crimes, they would abandon their course. So would all the evil little men— the criminals, the thieves and the kidnapers.

When the present moment and the immediate object is all that concerns us, then the emphasis is on what we can get now. We write off everything else but the gain and glory of today. We abandon conscience. Christ becomes a relic of the past. The Bible is referred to as a religious opiate. Hence the tendency is to deny the claim of the future. We become indifferent to tomorrow. We laugh at the idea of judgment and retribution. We conveniently idealize the future in terms of an empty vacuum. We construct a comfortable idea of God as a God of love without justice. In this oblivion of untruth we live as we choose, unwilling to listen when the Bible speaks, "It is appointed unto man once to die, but after this the judgment" or to heed when it says, "Be sure your sin will find you out."

We have taken an unnatural and wholly illogical attitude to death. Naturally, there is no satisfactory understanding of death, except by the Christian meaning of life.

One of our columnists writes: "The mother of a friend of mine died the other day. My friend's eleven-year-old daughter was sent away until after the funeral. She must be spared the knowledge of death.

"Is this not characteristic of our society? We treat death as if it were an aberration. Age approaches, but beautician, *masseur* and gland specialist co-operate to keep alive the illusion that we are not really growing

older. Anything that reminds us of the inescapable fact
that we are to die seems morbid to us.''

As for the Christian, death is not a conclusion—it is
a transition; the grave is not permanent—it is temporary.

In the almost unspeakable experience of the Apostle
Paul we notice his reference to being out of the body. He
said, ''And I knew such a man, (whether in the body, or
out of the body, I cannot tell: God knoweth).'' He was
''caught up'' but whether caught up physically or spiritually, he was not aware.

Being unaware did not detract from the experience
itself. It proved one thing: namely, a person does not
require a body to be conscious. Paul was conscious, but
he was not conscious of having a body. Of course, he
knew he had a body and we further know that whatever
happened to Paul occurred outside of the body. In other
words, it was a spiritual experience rather than a physical one. His body was not translated or transported into
paradise. While his spirit was in paradise, his body
was at Lystra for the disciples had gathered around it
after his enemies had dragged it out of the city, supposing Paul to be dead.

This experience of Paul was related for more reasons
sphere, the person was in another. The body was in
Lystra and the person in paradise.

This experience of Paul is related for more reasons
than merely to refute his opponents. It was given as
a preview of what happens after the death of men and
women in Christ. Death releases us from our body and
places us in the presence of Christ. This release is
immediate and instantaneous. There is no punishment
in purgatory, nor unconsciousness in the grave.

Paul has already said, ''To be absent from the body
[is] to be present with the Lord.'' This means a transition from death to life, for if we are present with the
Lord, it is a conscious presence in life.

In Ephesians 3:15 Paul refers to "the whole family in heaven and earth." This family is God's family. It is the family of the twice-born. You notice this family is either in heaven or on earth. It does not say that some of them are sleeping in the grave in unconsciousness. It is true the bodies of many are, but not the persons. The person is in heaven and all whom death hath not yet touched are on earth.

There are but two places of being for a Christian who is a member of God's family, in heaven or on earth. Paul previewed heaven in his experience of violence at Lystra.

What kind of an experience did Paul have? Was he actually dead or only apparently dead? Was he unconscious or was he dead? Some say it was a state of coma, but in such a state where death has not occurred, it is unlikely that such an experience could take place. Modern science declares that there are two kinds of death. There is reversible death and irreversible death. In reversible death, men have been brought back to life. We have heard of recent cases where physicians have hypodermically injected a substance known as adrenalin into the heart, and it has re-stimulated that organ to action and the person not only revived, but survived an experience of reversible death.

Such apparently, was Paul's experience. It was more than a state of coma or unconsciousness. It was a state of reversible death wherein he experienced all the sensations of dying.

In this state he declared that he was "caught up into paradise, and heard unspeakable words, which it is not lawful for a man to utter." What he meant was that what he saw was beyond adequate description. Our words could not describe his experience. He could not describe his paradise-experience in his earth-language.

There was no common ground for either experience or expression.

These wonderful things were Paul's own experience. They were not communicated to him by an occult medium. He did not have to employ any of the tricks of the occultists. His experience was immediate and personal. It was direct and divine. It was not the case of spirits coming back to use the bodies and voices of men to give a message. None of the conditions of the so-called occult of our day were involved in Paul's experience.

Evidently it was an anticipation of heaven and the life which is to be. That life is now resident in the Christian. It is not something he will receive. He has already received it. In the consciousness and contentment of what he now possesses, he is able to say, "For I know whom I have believed, and am persuaded that he is able to keep that which I have committed unto him against that day."

Notice now how the scene of Paul's experience changed. The next phase of his experience was with pain. The scene of experience changed from heaven to earth.

It was from the clouds to the clods. Paul was made conscious of the reality of his present existence. He might have had his head in the clouds, but he was walking with his feet on the earth.

It was from the throne to the thorn. No doubt he would have delighted to continue the throne experience, but the thorn came lest he "should be exalted above measure through the abundance of the revelation."

It was from praise to pain. Paul had just been speaking of an experience too wonderful for utterance or adequate expression. Now he has descended to suffering which, except for the grace of God, was too great to bear.

Yes, there is both the glory-side and the gory-side to

our Christian experience. There is the mountain top and the valley. Without the confinement of the valley we would never appreciate the glorious vistas of the mountain top.

The Bible has much to say about suffering. Notice the hymnology of the Church. Its songs are filled with musical poems about suffering and pain. They are the collective cry of the human heart for solace and surcease. They seem to sense the need of the human spirit for understanding and help. All of the cries are grounded finally in the Scriptures where we find an adequate and satisfying answer to the problem of pain.

Scattered throughout the Scriptures we find a complete philosophy of suffering. This philosophy is not found in one place, but when gathered together it presents a complete picture.

We are indebted to Dr. A. T. Pierson for the following valuable collection of Scriptural facts on the Bible's philosophy of suffering:

1. The Retributive or Judicial (Romans 2:2-11).
2. The Administrative, or Organic and Hereditary (Exodus 20:5-6; Romans 5:12-21).
3. The Punitive or Penal (II Samuel 12:13-19; Hebrews 12:15-17).
4. The Corrective or Paternal (Hebrews 12:5-12).
5. The Educative or Disciplinary (Hebrews 2:10; I Peter 1:6-7).
6. The Vindicative or Exemplary (Job 1:12; Daniel 6; Ephesians 6:10-20).
7. The Redemptive, or Voluntary and Vicarious (Colossians 1:24).

The wealth of suggestion found here only deep study can reveal. Retributive suffering is the final judicial infliction of punishment upon the rebellious, impenitent, unbelieving. It may be wholly escaped by repentance, faith and self-surrender, so that the believer will never come into judgment.

What we have called the administrative pertains to God's method of administering human history. He has established an organic connection between parent and offspring, ancestry and posterity, and a corporate connection between members of the same society, or, as we significantly call it, "commonwealth," whereby the sins and follies, as also virtues and excellencies of the sire, are measurably entailed on the son; and if one member of the body politic suffer, all the members suffer with it; or if one be honored, all rejoice with it. To suspend this organic law would not only arrest the evil consequences of others' wrong doing, but prevent the blessings which are conveyed in the same channel. Hence our duty is to adjust ourselves to this law by such moderation of our indulgences and virtuousness of habit as both modify the evil consequences of parental sins, and prevent a like inheritance in our children.

By the punitive is meant suffering which even forgiveness does not wholly obviate or prayer remove. "God is not mocked: for whatsoever a man soweth, that shall he also reap." David's sin was put away, but the child born of it could not be spared. Esau's repentance and remorse could not undo the barter of his birthright, or recall the prophetic blessing that went with it. Nor could even Moses enter the land after his dishonoring of God at Meribah-Kadesh.

Corrective suffering is of the nature of paternal chastisement. It can be gotten rid of immediately by correcting the fault, for no father continues his chastisement when the child is penitent and obedient. Hence in I Corinthians 11:30-32, we are taught that "if we would judge ourselves, we should not be judged." It is our lack of self-correction that makes the Father's needful.

Suffering may likewise be educative, preparing us for service and maturing in us virtues only ripened in sorrow, like patience which obviously must be learned when there is something to be patient about, to be borne patiently. Even our Lord had to be perfected through such suffering, for the captain of a company prepares for his captaincy by enduring hardship as a good soldier, sharing the training with the members of his company. Gold can only be rid of alloy by furnace fires. It has three states of history: in the mine, in the firing pot or crucible, and in the vessel: and it gets to be in the vessel and on the master's table only by passing through the fire.

Vindicative suffering is what we endure in vindication of God, as Job did when the devil challenged Jehovah to produce a man that served Him without respect to temporal advantage. The Lord needed such a witness in Babylon and Daniel went into the lions' den to vindicate God by proving that a praying saint will not give up even his prayers or conceal them to save his life.

Redemptive suffering is that which is voluntarily endured to save others. In the nature of the case it must be voluntary in order to be truly vicarious. It is never compulsory, God puts no cross on us; if we bear it at all it is because we take it up after Christ. Paul could not atone for human guilt, nor redeem men, but he could fill up what was behind in the sufferings of Christ by identifying himself with t.e Redeemer in voluntary self-denial for His sake and bringing to the knowledge of the lost the fact of salvation. This suffering, so far from being evaded or avoided, should be regarded as the consummate privilege of the believer.

Many of us cling to the notion that life ought to be made to suit us. We feel that if adversity befalls us then unnatural evil has overtaken us. We may even think of life as an easy road for carefree wanderers of pleasure.

We must awaken to the fact that life is a struggle and

its greatest victories arise out of that fact. We must all continually remember that "there hath no temptation taken you but such as is common to man." It is also written that we are to "think it not strange concerning the fiery trial which is to try you, as though some strange thing happened unto you: but rejoice, inasmuch as ye are partakers of Christ's sufferings; that, when his glory shall be revealed, ye may be glad also with exceeding joy" (I Peter 4:12-13).

To what purpose and what cause then shall we attribute these experiences of pain? There is a purpose in their cause and a blessing to be found in their effect.

II. THE EXPERIENCE OF PAIN (verses 7-10)

And lest I should be exalted above measure through the abundance of the revelations, there was given to me a thorn in the flesh, the messenger of Satan to buffet me, lest I should be exalted above measure. For this thing I besought the Lord thrice, that it might depart from me. And he said unto me, My grace is sufficient for thee: for my strength is made perfect in weakness. Most gladly therefore will I rather glory in my infirmities, that the power of Christ may rest upon me. Therefore I take pleasure in infirmities, in reproaches, in necessities, in persecutions, in distresses for Christ's sake: for when I am weak, then am I strong.

We attribute most of our difficulties and adversities to unbelief as if lack of faith were the cause for these things. More often the cause is stubbornness.

There is a spiritual stubbornness in which people refuse to yield their tenacious desires. They insist that certain prayers be answered. They insist on their desires being granted, and on their plans being completed. Stubbornness of this kind is always fatal to a happy, contented and consistent Christian experience.

As we traverse the path of Paul's experience and go with him down into the valley of suffering, we do not look at Paul the great apostle, or Paul the Christian warrior, or Paul the great man of faith, or Paul the man of answered prayer. We see Paul the thorn-bearer and Paul the sufferer. It seems very significant that suffering of a permanent character should seize such a man as Paul. He was God's chosen apostle and if any one deserved by right of merit and by reason of usefulness to be free from suffering, certainly Paul did. He was a man of prayer and a man of faith. Yet with all these recommendations and all his ability and usefulness, Paul was a man of physical handicap and suffering.

To begin with, we must remember Paul was a much-maligned man. He had many enemies both inside and outside the church. There were false teachers who were denying the divine apostleship of Paul. Perhaps one of the things cited to prove this was Paul's thorn. They probably pointed the finger of scorn and said that Paul was a fine apostle sent from God, and that had he been such, then God would heal him by removing the thorn.

Has any one ever pointed the finger of scorn at your thorn and said, "A fine Christian! Look at all the trouble you have. Look at your difficulties. Look at all your enemies. Were you genuine, you would not have any trouble."

Well, if that has not happened to you, you may be sure it has to many who may be like you. It certainly occurred to Paul and out of its occurrence comes this remarkable teaching of finding advantage in adversity.

We have six points to consider in this passage.

A. *Paul's Thorn* (verse 7)

... there was given me a thorn in the flesh ...

To begin with, Paul's pain was caused by a "thorn in the flesh." The word used here means a "palisade" or a pointed stake used for impaling victims. It is used as a metaphor to describe Paul's impalement by pain. It was a living crucifixion and is so described in Way's translation of this verse: "Yes, and in the matter of these very revelations—lest through the transcendent splendor of them I might be over-elated—there was given to me that which tortured me like a stake driven through the flesh.''

It must have been something possessing reality and is to be judged by the senses. It was not an illusion or a mere mental concept or an erroneous idea. It belonged to the category of demonstrable existence. It was not personal imagination nor a creation of the mind. It had substance. Did you ever sit on a thorn? How did you react? Did you remain still without the flash of an eyelash and say to yourself that all you were sitting on was the error of your mind? The normal reaction to a thorn is the physical sensation of pain and the muscular reaction of movement.

Yes, Paul's thorn was a reality and if the language which describes it means anything, it was suffering with a point.

The question is invariably raised as to the particular nature of Paul's thorn. Some say it was the opposition of his enemies; others, that it was a temptation. Still others say it was a moral weakness, but none of these answer the question satisfactorily.

The Bible plainly states it was a ''thorn in the flesh.'' It is wresting the whole sense of the passage to say that this flesh is the flesh of Paul's moral nature. It must have been the flesh of his physical nature. It was something in his body. It produced bodily sensations.

Galatians 4:14-15 seems to give us our only clue to the identification of this physical thorn. ''And my temptation which was in my flesh ye despised not, nor rejected; but received me as an angel of God, even as Christ Jesus. Where is then the blessedness ye spake of? for I bear you record, that, if it had been possible, ye would have plucked out your own eyes, and have given them to me.''

Combine two clauses of these two verses, ''And my

temptation which was in my flesh'' and ''Ye would have plucked out your own eyes, and have given them to me'' and you have a very reasonable idea of his affliction. Then, too, when Paul finished this letter to the Galatians he said, ''Ye see how large a letter I have written unto you with mine own hand.'' It was not the size of the epistle, but the size of the characters he used in writing. He had to use large bold characters because of the optical deficiency from which he suffered.

His eye trouble may have been ophthalmia which is inflammation of the eyeball, or trachoma which produces a granulation of the eyelids. At any rate it was something which caused constant pain, discomfort and disability.

B. *Pain's Source* (verse 7)

. . . the messenger of Satan . . .

This is the most inexplicable part of the whole experience.

Satan and not God is the source of evil and suffering. They are allowed to touch us in the natural course of human life and by the permissive will of God.

C. *Pain's Purpose* (verse 7)

. . . to buffet me, lest I should be exalted above measure.

The most dangerous and destructive form of pride is spiritual pride. There is social pride, place pride, fashion pride and class pride. There are other kinds of pride, but the deadliest is spiritual pride.

Paul's pain was a form of preventive suffering. The spiritual constitution of the greatest of apostles and the greatest of saints was apparently too weak to sustain the effect of the unspeakable revelations he had experienced, and God permitted the thorn as a preventive against spiritual pride. This is what Paul meant when he wrote ''to buffet me, lest I should be exalted above

measure.'' ''To buffet'' is an expression which means
to strike with the hands or fist, or literally, to maltreat
by a continual succession of body blows.

''Above measure'' is an expression which means ''too
much.'' It implies that there is a legitimate measure
of exaltation for us to enjoy. Christian experience is
not a system of either physical or spiritual asceticism.
It does not require the abuse of the flesh for the development of the spirit. It is designed to give a proper expression of the emotions. Exalted feelings have a safe
limit but there is such a thing as being exalted ''above
measure.'' At this point spiritual pleasure becomes
spiritual pride and emotionalism becomes fanaticism.

Paul was content to suffer the bludgeonings of these
buffetings, knowing their beneficent effect.

D. *Paul's Desire* (verse 8)

For this thing I besought the Lord thrice, that it might depart
from me.

Paul's desire was normal. It was the natural reaction
to pain to desire its relief. Paul asked God for its
removal. It was not a casual religious request.

1. He Asked in Prayer.

Paul prayed for his healing. He believed in prayer
for the body as well as for the soul. He believed that
prayer was as efficacious in the practical necessities of
life as in any spiritual matter. In other words, prayer
had an object as well as a subject. Much of our praying
has only a subject. Its subject is words and phrases.
What is its object? Is it directed to specific conditions
and needs?

Men say, ''If God knows what we need, why ask Him
for it?'' People pray with all their might as if God
needed information or as if He needed to be coaxed into
acquiescence. The purpose of prayer is not to coax
God into doing what we want, or to try to change His

will. Instead, it is to help us to find out what God's will for us is.

2. He Asked in Faith

Faith is not something which forces God to do what we want. Instead, it is something which unites us with the source of divine energy and blessing.

3. He Asked with Persistence

Paul said he "besought the Lord thrice." It was the perfect proportion of persistence. He was not weak in faith so that he stopped after the first denial of his desire. Nor was he stubborn about it that he continued praying a purely selfish petition. We notice that he prayed thrice and then stopped praying. He did not pray for years for what might be known to a full measure of faith. Paul undoubtedly knew what God's will was. In this respect his prayer was answered although his request was denied. If prayer's purpose is to discover God's will, then that purpose was realized.

Because all these conditions—namely, prayer, faith and persistence—prevailed, we cannot say that the continuance of Paul's thorn was in the lack of Paul's spiritual experience. Neither need we assume the same thing in our own experience when these things are present. We need to consider God's higher purpose.

E. *God's Answer* (verse 9)

And he said unto me, My grace is sufficient for thee: for my strength is made perfect in weakness.

God's answer was not in accordance with Paul's expressed desire but with God's will. His will and not our desire is the governing factor in prayer.

However, God did answer, not by removing the thorn so as to make it easy for Paul, but rather by giving sufficient grace for the bearing of his thorn.

Why should this be? Why does not God remove my

disability instead of giving me grace? It would be just as easy for Him to give one answer as the other. The reason is discipline, power and perfection.

On certain kinds of clocks there are clock weights. These weights keep the clock going. The very difficulties which beset us will prove to be incentives to prayer and perseverance, and the means by which God will become more real and the avenue over which a whole new kind of spiritual experience will open up to us.

The railroads use a device known as the derail. It lies on the track for the purpose of throwing off the wheels of the locomotive. Its intention is not to cause a wreck, but to protect other trains. God has derailing devices. When we need the sidetrack for repairs or correction, yet willfully go against His caution and danger signals, He has means of derailing us. These are the stops which are as necessary for our well-being as the starts.

In such cases chastening is not necessarily punishment. It is still true that "whom the Lord loveth he chasteneth." Chastening refines and improves. It is not given to condemn or restrain. Because this is so, sickness is not necessarily the result of wrongdoing, or the consequence of sin. Jesus said of the blind man, "Neither hath this man sinned, nor his parents: but that the works of God should be made manifest in him."

It is not true that all chastening comes through thorns in the flesh. It may be heartache, the perfidy of friends, misrepresentation, disappointment, losses or sorrow. These may be necessary because none of us are practically perfect. We may be positionally perfect, but not practically so. Because of this, chastening becomes the crucible of character.

Knowing this, we shall be armed with understanding and shall endure with patience believing that "he which hath begun a good work in [us] will perform it until the day of Jesus Christ.''

We have striven for an answer to the ever present problem of pain and misfortune. In seeking that answer we must be careful to observe Scriptural distinctions. For us the answer is not in the Old Testament because that is outside our present dispensational realm. The experience of Paul is the dispensational answer to our present problem of sickness, suffering and so-called misfortune of all kinds.

There are unwarranted opinions to the effect that sickness and trouble in the Christian are the result of sin. If that is so, Paul was a sinner and the account we have in this incident is the story of personal sin. It is unthinkable! If it was so, Paul was a sinner in the midst of a great and abundant service, in the midst of prayer and in the midst of great faith. If such is sin, then it is a new kind of sinning and Paul was a blessed kind of sinner.

We dare not go to the other extreme of fatalism and say that sickness and suffering are inevitable. There is a wise providence behind Christian experience. The purposes of this providence do not always appear to us. The effect of this providence we cannot always understand nor even appreciate. Nevertheless it is there.

F. *Paul's Attitude* (verses 9-10)

Most gladly therefore will I rather glory in my infirmities, that the power of Christ may rest upon me. Therefore I take pleasure in infirmities, in reproaches, in necessities, in persecutions, in distresses for Christ's sake: for when I am weak, then am I strong.

God's answer to Paul's desire was not the subtraction of Paul's pain but the addition of God's grace. He replied to Paul's thrice-repeated prayer, ''My grace is sufficient for thee.''

You will notice two ''therefore's.''

1. ''Therefore will I rather glory in my infirmi-

ties, that the power of Christ may rest upon me'' (verse 9).

   2.   ''Therefore I take pleasure in infirmities, in reproaches, in necessities, in persecutions, in distresses for Christ's sake: for when I am weak, then am I strong'' (verse 10).

Here is the key to the problem of suffering. It is Paul's attitude. It is not God's answer in granting Paul's desire, but Paul's attitude in accepting God's answer.

It was not a changed attitude about the reality of suffering. Paul did not come to believe it was unreal and nonexistent. He still believed in a practical Christian realism. Sin was still sinful and sickness painful.

Paul's attitude about the certainty of suffering was not changed. That would be fatalism and fatalism has no part in faith. Instead, it was a change in attitude about God's purpose. That was faith.

Paul was not gloating over and glorying in rotting corpuscles or broken bones or failing eyesight when he said, ''Most gladly therefore will I rather glory in my infirmities.'' He was glorying in the fact that the infirmity was, in God's purpose, to be the medium of something greater. This something greater was power. It was that ''the power of Christ may rest upon me.''

There may be a so-called painless dentistry, but there is no such force as painless power. Whatever kind of power you name, you will find it to be something which is developed at an expense. It requires pressure, fire, constriction and tribulation. Water power comes from the pressure of accumulated masses of water backed up by a dam and forced through turbines which generate electricity. Steam power comes by fire which heats water until it expands and creates pressure in a cylinder. Electric power is by constriction which acts by a negative and positive current, causing motion. Gasoline power is the explosion of volatile gasoline in a chamber called a cylinder, where that exploded gasoline expands and pushes the cylinder head to create motion.

In a similar fashion in the spiritual sphere, physical suffering and mental anguish create pressure that produce power. Whoever wants power must have pressure. Even the power of the Holy Spirit is not an impersonal surge of feeling. All who really know it have felt it. Here Paul expressed a great truth when he gloried in infirmities, for they meant power.

It is very important to connect the glorying with the suffering. If we merely suffer it may only mean the endurance of pain. When we glory in suffering it means preparation for power. The key to suffering is our attitude to it. Change your groaning to glorying and you will exchange your pain for power.

Do not forget the importance of the changed attitude. It is the secret of suffering. Trees are made limber so they may bend in the wind, otherwise they would snap off and break. It is our pliability in pain that will give us ease and comfort. When we are willfully unbending and refuse to yield and stand up to our pain with an uncompromising attitude, we suffer all the more.

We can scarcely fathom the tremendous depth of Paul's attitude to suffering when he said, "Therefore I take pleasure in infirmities, in reproaches, in necessities, in persecutions, in distresses for Christ's sake: for when I am weak, then am I strong."

You will notice that besides physical infirmities he named "reproaches"—this is mental; "necessities"—this is economic; "persecutions"—this is social; "distresses"—this is emotional. When his attitude to these was pleasure, then their effect was strength.

To be strong in weakness is a paradox of Christian experience. It is one of the most valuable lessons we can ever learn. We have a mistaken idea of strength

of character. The strongest are not necessarily they
who can defend themselves against others. To be self-
sufficient we assume that we must avenge our wrongs,
carry our point, demand justice, but to be Christ-suffi-
cient we are strong when we are weak. "True strength
is the overpowering of divine love. Love is always
strong. It dwells with holiness and righteousness and
truth. It is strong enough to be meek. Many have mistaken meekness for weakness, forgetting that it is a
mark of superior strength to bear evil and refuse to
retaliate. With strength is found quietness and calm-
ness of spirit. He who has found the strength of the
Lord can wait patiently while God works His will."

The story has been told of a man who made a clock
and showed it to a friend who had never seen one before.
The fashioner of the clock opened the back of it and
asked the man what he thought of its maker. The man
saw some big wheels and other small ones, some wheels
going one way and others the opposite way and some
wheels going slowly and others fast. Seeing this confusion he answered, "I think the man who made that is
mad." Then the maker took his friend to the front side
of the clock and asked what he now thought of its maker.
The man looked at the two hands of the clock moving
smoothly and regularly, each one in its appointed circle
and both of them telling perfectly the time of day, and
he replied, "I think the man who made that is the wisest
person who ever lived."

This story gives us a glimpse of a profound truth.
The fault of our thinking arises from the fact that we
stand on earth on the wrong side of God's providences,
and thus fail to see His perfect designing. One day we
shall stand on the right side and then we shall understand. In the meantime, God asks us to believe, even
though we do not understand.

We have no right to think that infirmity, whether it

is a case of pain, handicap or circumscribed economical circumstances, exempts us from activity. Infirmity is never an excuse for inactivity.

We notice that Paul was plunged from privilege to pain. We saw him in his incomparable experience of glory exalted to the third heaven. Immediately thereafter we see him suffering the thorn in his flesh. We see him in infirmities, in reproaches, in necessities, in persecutions and in distresses. His privileges did not exempt him from pain. In fact, his privileges increased his pain because it was divine intention to keep him on an even keel. Pain was to balance privilege. Were it all privilege, it would bring pride. Were it all pain, it would bring despair. It is both in order to bring equality and equilibrium.

Now we shall see that Paul moved from pain to practice; from suffering to service. He was taken from the bed to the bench.

III. The Experience of Practice (verses 11-21)

The substance of this Scripture portion is expressed in a simple sentence. We are either helping or hindering the cause of Christ. Between these two, lies no middle ground of neutrality. To be inactive does not necessarily mean that we are ineffective. Our very activity may be a hinderance to Christ's cause.

A. *The Answer to Accusation* (verses 11-12)

I am become a fool in glorying; ye have compelled me: for I ought to have been commended of you: for in nothing am I behind the very chiefest apostles, though I be nothing. Truly the signs of an apostle were wrought among you in all patience, in signs, and wonders, and mighty deeds.

Paul was not a spurious servant. His apostleship was accompanied by genuineness. There was fruit in his ministry. He justified his claims by presenting a record of signs, wonders and mighty deeds.

These were apostolic signs. The signs of discipleship need not necessarily include wonders and mighty deeds, but they must include fruits. The fruits of an apostle and a disciple may be different in their extent, but not in their character, for all are to be a justification of the reality of our profession and a proper contribution to the cause and the Christ we serve.

B. *The Blessing of Helping* (verses 13-19)

For what is it wherein ye were inferior to other churches, except it be that I myself was not burdensome to you? forgive me this wrong. Behold, the third time I am ready to come to you; and I will not be burdensome to you: for I seek not your's, but you: for the children ought not to lay up for the parents, but the parents for the children. And I will very gladly spend and be spent for you; though the more abundantly I love you, the less I be loved. But be it so, I did not burden you: nevertheless, being crafty, I caught you with guile. Did I make a gain of you by any of them whom I sent unto you? I desired Titus, and with him I sent a brother. Did Titus make a gain of you? walked we not in the same spirit? walked we not in the same steps? Again, think ye that we excuse ourselves unto you? we speak before God in Christ: but we do all things, dearly beloved, for your edifying.

Paul had noble motives in his service. For instance, he said, ''I seek not your's, but you.'' He was not serving the people because he was interested in their property. His interest was in them and not in what they had. He sought their salvation and their growth and in seeking these things he realized a satisfying profit.

Again he said, ''We do all things, dearly beloved, for your edifying.'' His labors were not for the reward of a wage. They were extended to promote the spiritual progress of the church.

We should never think of ministers as being hired. They are to be supported. Hiring commercializes a sacred function, but support is the spontaneous response of grateful hearts.

The idea of any kind of money support or gift or reward for a Christian worker is repugnant to many. In fact, there are people who think any mention of money in connection with any kind of Christian service is an evidence of religious racketeering. However, religious racketeering is not necessarily in the asking for money but in the employment of it. Any legitimate Christian work must have support for its needs. Judge it by the use it makes of that which it receives.

Paul found himself making the mistake of not asking. This left the benefactors of his ministry without the proportionate responsibility of sharing. He said in verse 13, "For what is it wherein ye were inferior to other churches, except it be that I myself was not burdensome to you? forgive me this wrong." Notice this request, "Forgive me this wrong." He had wronged them in sparing them from supporting him.

Ruskin said, "The law of nature is, that a certain quantity of work is necessary to produce a certain quantity of good of any kind whatever. If you want knowledge, you must toil for it; if food, you must toil for it and if pleasure, you must toil for it." Receiving requires giving and when Paul exempted the Corinthians from supporting him in his labors for them, he wronged them. Their support would have eased Paul's labors and released him for wider and more extensive spiritual activities. It would also have caused the Corinthians to have a greater appreciation of what they had received. What costs us nothing is appreciated in the same manner.

Usually, those who make the most strenuous objections to their legitimate responsibility as stewards are those who have a faulty appreciation of their opportunities.

If it is true that whoever receives must give, it is also true that whoever gives creates a larger capacity to receive. That is what Paul meant when he said, "Forgive me this wrong." He had wronged them by relieving them of responsibility. Being thus relieved they settled back in selfish enjoyment of Paul's ministry. If they had been made to share his support, they would have prized his service and expanded their own capacity for spiritual things. Is it not true that whoever works to provide his own food has by his very labor created an appetite to enjoy it? The person who is fed without the expenditure of effort or money is done an injustice. There cannot possibly be a proper appreciation.

It is time all of us inquired how Christ's blessings have caused us to respond. What have we to give? What have we done? To what reciprocal measure have we extended ourselves in return for our blessings?

Paul revealed the fallacy of relieving the Corinthians of reciprocal responsibility when he said in verse 15, "... though the more abundantly I love you, the less I be loved." Lavished love without required labor brought a distorted view of life. Thus the more he loved, the less they loved. Had he required responsibility at their hand, he would have received a higher measure of appreciation.

The very nature of Christianity requires a reciprocal giving, service and useful occupation. "We are his workmanship, created in Christ Jesus unto good works." Notice that we are "created in Christ Jesus unto good works." The goal of the Christian life is neither to escape hell or to gain heaven. Of course these are true, but the supreme object is the production of our lives for good.

The Bible teaches us trust in God. This is something utterly foreign to many people. When emergencies arise and danger is imminent, they have no personal recourse to faith in God.

"There was a heavy storm at sea and a nervous woman passenger went to the captain. 'Captain,' she asked, 'are we in great danger?' 'Madam,' he replied, 'we are in the hands of God.' 'Oh,' she exclaimed, 'is it as bad as that?'"

The opposite of this story of an adult's **desperate**

plight and futile attitude to God is another story about a little girl in England.

"Rosemary, one of the many little girls recently sent out of London, was going to bed on her first evening in the country. 'Do you say your prayers before going to bed, darling?' her hostess asked. Rosemary said she did. 'Well, then, kneel down and I'll listen as your mother does.' Rosemary repeated the usual 'Now I lay me down to sleep' and then improvised a postscript of her own. 'And God, please protect Daddy and Mommy from those German bombs. And, do, dear God, take care of Yourself—because if anything happens to You, we're sunk'."

The epistle of Second Corinthians teaches us the importance of a sensible spiritual experience. It has led us through the varied experiences of life. It has taken us from the heights to the depths. It has brought us through the valley of providential pain where God's answer to the pleading sufferer was sufficient grace. Instead of taking away pain, God gave overcoming power. This is so because God has sometimes a purpose we do not see.

Besides providential pain which causes distress we find the record of experiences of our own folly which create suffering among God's people.

C. *The Handicap of Hindering* (verses 20-21)

For I fear, lest, when I come, I shall not find you such as I would, and that I shall be found unto you such as ye would not: lest there be debates, envyings, wraths, strifes, backbitings, whisperings, swellings, tumults: and lest, when I come again, my God will humble me among you, and that I shall bewail many which have sinned already, and have not repented of the uncleanness and fornication and lasciviousness which they have committed.

James said, "My brethren, count it all joy when ye fall into divers temptations." There is a difference between falling into these experiences and walking into them.

What Paul feared for the Corinthians was that which resulted from the folly of their own carnality.

These verses are translated by Way to read: "I dread, oh, I dread lest, when I do visit you, I may find a disappointing change in you, and that you may find a disappointing change in me. I dread lest I may find among you dissensions, jealousy, stormy passions, intrigues, slanders, malicious gossip, inflated conceit, turbulence. I dread lest, when I come this next time, God may humiliate me at the sight of you. I dread lest I may have to mourn over many who have previously lived in sin, and yet have never repented of the uncleanness, the fornication, the wantonness which they have practiced."

These are the things that hinder. We are either helpers or hinderers. We are either wings or weights. It might serve us well if we were brave enough to deal with our own hearts with severity to determine which category we are in.

Paul gave us a list of eight unholy things which threaten to destroy the Church of any and all times. You will notice that none of these sins is a flagrant vice. They are not the violent sins of the flesh, but those vicious sins of the carnal disposition. These sins are destructive to the peace of the church. They cause dissensions that result in divisions.

Remember, this Scripture is talking about sin among Christians. There is such a thing. Until this is dealt with and corrected, there can be scant hope of effectively dealing with sin in the world.

These are the dispositional sins.

Debates. I know no simpler definition than "common, ordinary fussing." So many people go around with their carnality grown out at their elbow!

Envyings. Few are capable of the magnanimous spirit of rejoicing in another's success and blessing.

Wraths. This is the accumulated effect and explosive

end of debates and envyings. It is the bitter result of carnal wrangling.

Strifes. This is the display of stormy passions and the consequent disturbance of peace.

Backbitings and Whisperings. These undoubtedly refer to secret slander and vicious innuendo that cast suspicion on a brother. It is the sabotage of character and the work of moral fifth columnists.

Swellings. What a picturesque description this is! It refers to inflated conceit like the pouting of a pigeon or the swelling of a frog. How little it takes to deflate an inflated frog and how little he becomes after the vacuous wind of conceit is gone!

Tumults. These are the concurrent disturbances resulting from the preceding sins.

Paul expressed anxiety lest these continue to pollute the sanctuary.

What was worse, was the fact that these very people were the ones who were finding fault with Paul's preaching against sin. Their agitation against him was to smother the voice of a guilty conscience within. Guilt seeks to divert condemnation in the sinner by directing criticism toward the servant.

13

THE COMMENDATION OF HONESTY
2 Corinthians 13

Life endures! There is a life that meets all foes with triumph. There is a life that faces disaster with conquest. There is a life that supplies us with the necessary elements of existence. There is a life that is indispensable. That life is the life of Christ.

The Christian life is not merely an improvement on human life. The spiritual life is not an advanced step beyond the natural life. It is something unique and different. It begins in a moment and lasts through eternity. It requires a birth that begets a new creature. This very epistle says, "Therefore if any man be in Christ, he is a new creature: old things are passed away; behold, all things are become new."

This new life is immediately faced with old problems. It marches into the arena of human conflict where the age-old disputes, distresses, diseases and disasters are thrown against it.

The apostle, whose autobiographical account this letter is, ran the gamut of human experience. He met and mastered every kind of foe. He did it, not as Saul of Tarsus, but as Paul the disciple and apostle of Jesus Christ. He did it not as a philosopher, scientist or religionist, but as a Christian.

Since this epistle deals with so wide a variety of experience and since it shows us the applicability of Christianity to those experiences, it consequently shows the proximity of God to our problems.

If we could be persuaded that God is where our problem is, we would have the confidence that gives victorious living, but how few of us are confident of that fact. We think in vague religious terms instead of in terms of a personal God. We think in terms of a church instead of a Christ. We think in terms of liturgy instead of life.

One day the telephone in the office of the rector of President Roosevelt's Washington church rang, and an eager voice said, "Tell me, do you expect the President to be in church this Sunday?" "That," the rector explained patiently, "I cannot promise. But we expect God to be there, and we fancy that will be incentive enough for a reasonably large attendance."

Yes, He will, but God will also be in your home. He is not restricted to a church. Our bodies are temples of divine residence and operation. We do not have to go to a church building for God's blessing. If we are new creatures we have the new basis for life. This new basis for life means a life that endures under assault, pressure, disaster, tribulation. It means a new freedom.

Madame Guyon was imprisoned in the lonely and miserable Bastille for her Christian testimony, yet she sang:

> Stone walls do not a prison make,
>   Nor iron bars a cage;
> Minds innocent and quiet take
>   That for an hermitage;
> If I have freedom in my love,
>   And in my soul am free,
> Angels alone that soar above
>   Enjoy such liberty.

This new basis of life means:

A New Meaning of Comfort (1:3-4)

Blessed be God, even the Father of our Lord Jesus Christ, the Father of mercies, and the God of all comfort; who comforteth us in all our tribulation, that we may be able to comfort them which are in any trouble, by the comfort wherewith we ourselves are comforted of God.

A New Meaning of Influence (2:15)

For we are unto God a sweet savour of Christ, in them that are saved, and in them that perish.

A New Meaning of the Christian Life (3:18)

But we all, with open face beholding as in a glass the glory of the Lord, are changed into the same image from glory to glory, even as by the Spirit of the Lord.

A New Meaning of Affliction (4:17)

For our light affliction, which is but for a moment, worketh for us a far more exceeding and eternal weight of glory.

A New Meaning of Death (5:1)

For we know that if our earthly house of this tabernacle were dissolved, we have a building of God, an house not made with hands, eternal in the heavens.

A New Meaning of Service (6:3-5)

Giving no offence in any thing, that the ministry be not blamed: but in all things approving ourselves as the ministers of God, in much patience, in afflictions, in necessities, in distresses, in stripes, in imprisonments, in tumults, in labours, in watchings, in fastings.

A New Meaning of Holiness (7:1)

Having therefore these promises, dearly beloved, let us cleanse ourselves from all filthiness of the flesh and spirit, perfecting holiness in the fear of God.

A New Meaning of the Incarnation (8:9)

For ye know the grace of our Lord Jesus Christ, that, though he was rich, yet for your sakes he became poor, that ye through his poverty might be rich.

A New Meaning of Stewardship (9:7)

Every man according as he purposeth in his heart, so let him give; not grudgingly, or of necessity: for God loveth a cheerful giver.

A New Meaning of Warfare (10:4)

For the weapons of our warfare are not carnal, but mighty through God to the pulling down of strong holds.

A New Meaning of Chastening (11:30)

If I must needs glory, I will glory of the things which concern mine infirmities.

A New Meaning of Sickness (12:7-9)

And lest I should be exalted above measure through the abundance of the revelations, there was given to me a thorn in the flesh, the messenger of Satan to buffet me, lest I should be exalted above measure. For this thing I besought the Lord thrice, that it might depart from me. And he said unto me, My grace is sufficient for thee: for my strength is made perfect in weakness. Most gladly therefore will I rather glory in my infirmities, that the power of Christ may rest upon me.

A New Meaning of Personal Honesty (13:5)

Examine yourselves, whether ye be in the faith; prove your own selves. Know ye not your own selves, how that Jesus Christ is in you, except ye be reprobates?

In examining this remarkable account of Christianity at work in life, we do not find it discussed in terms of sectarianism. It is a wholesome and vigorous Christianity. Paul made no effort to gather glory for himself. He was not anxious to put a fence of personal possession around his experiences and put up a sign "No Trespassing." He did not ask us to be Paulites.

It is dangerous to personalize our experiences and assume that unless others have had duplicates they are not Christians. Sectarianism has produced grotesque interpretations and applications of Christianity.

Dr. John McNeill imagines that the blind man, whose healing is described in John 9:6-11 met the blind man of whose healing we are told in Luke 18:35-43. They had a little praise meeting for eyesight received, then the first blind man said to the second, "Of course the Lord took a little mud and put it on your eyes, and said, 'Now see.'" "No," replied the other, "He simply said, 'Receive thy sight' and I saw." "No, indeed," said the first, "if He did not put mud on your eyes, you are still as blind as a bat, because that is the way He healed me!" The argument went on. "And there and then," said Dr. McNeill, "the first two sects in the church began—the Mudites and the Anti-mudites."

When we have finished Second Corinthians we will
have dealt with a life which is in the magnificent proportions of Jesus Christ. It is neither Paul's version nor
conception. It is neither personal nor partisan.

There remains but one thing for us to do. Let us take
this enduring life into our existing problems. Let it go
to work for us and let us go to work for God.

Paul prepared to give his final admonitions to the
Christians of Corinth. He gave these admonitions in
the light of an anticipated visit which he was to make
to them. Because of this visit his letter had the purpose
of seeking the correction of their troubles so that his
visit might not be a punitive mission. He wanted it to
be pleasant. He wanted to be able to preach and not
punish. He wanted to feed them and minister to them.
It was with this in mind that he wrote unto them.

The thing Paul desired of all members of the Corinthian Church is a reality of experience that would give
them not only a correct profession but an honest and
straightforward appearance before the world.

His farewell remarks cover these points:

   I. The Urgency of Correction (verses 1-4)
   II. The Need of Self-Examination (verses 5-10)
   III. The Benediction of Farewell (verses 11-14)

   I. The Urgency of Correction (verses 1-4)

This is the third time I am coming to you. In the mouth of two
or three witnesses shall every word be established. I told you before,
and foretell you, as if I were present, the second time; and being
absent now I write to them which heretofore have sinned, and to all
other, that, if I come again, I will not spare: since ye seek a proof
of Christ speaking in me, which to you-ward is not weak, but is
mighty in you. For though he was crucified through weakness, yet
he liveth by the power of God. For we also are weak in him, but we
shall live with him by the power of God toward you.

Paul reminded them of the proximity of his visit. It
would be "the third time."

Paul's third visit promised severity in his dealing with both those who had sinned and those who suffered their sinning. He was prepared to exert the full force of his authority and power.

Most of us postpone the performance of needful duties until we are under the pressure of compulsion. Many people neglect the care of their health until disease is upon them. We do not like to pay our taxes until the eleventh hour. We keep confessions we ought to make until we are forced to make them.

How much better it would be if we were not dilatory in these matters. How much better it would have been for all concerned had the Corinthians dealt with their problems when they first arose. It would have saved Paul the great concern he bore for them. It would have spared them wasted years and vain regrets. Repairs are better mended when the break is fresh. Spiritual lesions and wounds are most easily healed in their earliest stages.

It may be that you have some personal business of this kind to take care of. An old wound, laid bare when friends parted, may need healing. A confession needs to be made—a correction of some wrong you have committed. It could be one of many things that you have waited to do. Do not wait too long. Do not wait until it is too late. Do not wait until God must use severe measures of correction. Do not wait until the third time; do it the first time.

Paul appealed to a Gospel principle which we quite generally overlook. He stated it in verse 4. "For we also are weak in him, but we shall live with him by the power of God toward you."

The Gospel possesses a power which rests in Christ. The power of Christ becomes power in the Christian. It is the power of death and life, for it speaks of Christ's dying by crucifixion and living by resurrection. The crucifixion was in weakness; the resurrection in power.

In speaking of the Cross in his first letter, Paul said to these Corinthians, ''For the preaching of the cross is to them that perish foolishness; but unto us which are saved it is the power of God.'' To the world of culture and power as represented in Greece and Rome, the Gospel of the Cross was both foolishness and weakness. It was utter foolishness and the most abject weakness that the world's Redeemer and moral leader should submit Himself to the death of the Cross. However, this very fact is the strength of Christianity. ''Because the foolishness of God is wiser than men; and the weakness of God is stronger than men.''

How can God be foolish and weak? The reality of it is impossible. It is only the apparent foolishness and weakness of God which is true. It is only true in the judgment of men when they view the Cross. By their standards the preaching of the Cross is foolishness. They refer to its simplicity. It is not erudite enough. It is not philosophic enough. The very simplicity of it is the secret and the strength of it.

It was not designed for man's head but for his needs. It was not intended to be a system of education, but regeneration. It was not made for man at his best, but at his worst. Therefore it must be simple, elementary and fundamental. Because of its simplicity it is wiser and more effective than all the philosophy and cultured reasoning of man. The simple preaching of Jesus has outlived the brilliant wisdom of the wise. Who remembers sentences from Seneca or portions from Plato? Similarly, the simple teachings of the Bible have outlived the entire writings of mankind. How many take enough interest in the sayings of Socrates to commit passage after passage to memory? They do it with the Bible. Bible portions sufficient to reconstruct the whole Book are stored away in minds all over the world. If every copy of the Bible could be destroyed today, you could rewrite it from the memories of Christians.

By men's standards, the Cross is a display of weakness. Jesus was born of peasants instead of the ruling class. He was an artisan instead of an aristocrat. He spurned the usual methods of achieving success. He did not use force. He did not have an elaborate organization. He was not a politician. He did not cater to public favor. When the crisis of His career came, He did not answer when falsely accused. He did not fight with the usual weapons of man. However, He was not impotent. His apparent weakness was only His unwillingness to use unworthy weapons. Nevertheless, His weakness was His strength. He ruled by love and not by law. He conquered by faith and not by force. He has survived and surmounted all the vaunted leaders of the world.

Modern dictators should have considered history before attempting world conquest, for the records show how futile are their methods. In *Parade* of September, 1940, appeared this article about Napoleon:

All Europe cowered at Napoleon's feet . . . He swept nations before him like chaff before the wind; he galvanized a whole continent into movement at his nod; he hurled armies over deserts and over mountain ranges. The marvel of this man's personality and of the power that emanated from him grows when we remember that there were no telegrams, no steamers, no railroads, no radios in those days, and yet in a world of slow movement and retarded communication Napoleon pervaded and shaped and molded the world as a potter the clay. He crashed his way to Berlin; he swept through Italy; "I shall be in Vienna in a month," he declared—and was there in three weeks; he rushed to Madrid and set up there a Corsican dynasty. But there Wellington grimly held the trenches . . .

At last it was not the Russians that defeated him. Fire and snow and frost and hunger—these, the elemental, undefeatable forces were his executioners. "God Almighty has been too much for me," he said when he was laid low at last. God was too much for him; defeated by the elemental, undefeatable forces he was; and Marshal Foch wrote of him: "He failed, they say, because he was without Berthier. I do not think so. In 1814 it is explained that he was already ill. Perhaps. But in my view the deep reason for the disaster that overwhelmed him must be sought elsewhere. He forgot that a man cannot be God; that above the individual there is the nation; that above man there is the moral law.

One of the most challenging considerations awaits our attention as we scan the last few sentences of this epistle to the Corinthians.

Paul wrote, "Examine yourselves." Our lives require our personal inspection and introspection. We are to be brave enough to survey ourselves with the scrutiny of sincerity. Oftentimes this scrutiny is postponed until it is too late; then we are called upon to pass through the fire of judgment and correction.

It is reported that in the very first newspaper published in Paris after the German occupation, there was printed in terms not customary to us, this remarkable statement and a six-column heading:

We are going to pay for sixty years of dechristianization, falling birth rate, decline into paganism and materialism, decline into political anarchy. We are paying dearly for the errors and crimes of our great French Revolution of 1789-99. Providence granted us twenty-five years respite in which to recover ourselves. We returned to our free-thinking, materialistic vomit, to our "popular front" moral and political anarchy. We have worn out the patience of Providence! We have disgusted the good God Himself; and now, when will the Lord grant us the recovery and resurrection of France?

Yes, France failed to make a national examination before it was too late. It took the smashing of her vaunted Maginot Line and the rumble of tanks under her Arc de Triomphe to awaken her to regret and repentance.

How much will it take to awaken us? Has God been whispering and then thundering in our consciences? Must the artillery and armory of divine judgment rumble through our lives before we will awake? God forbid!

II. The Need of Self-Examination (verses 5-10)

Examine yourselves, whether ye be in the faith; prove your own selves. Know ye not your own selves, how that Jesus Christ is in you, except ye be reprobates? But I trust that ye shall know that we are not reprobates. Now I pray to God that ye do no evil; not that we should appear approved, but that ye should do that which is honest, though we be as reprobates. For we can do nothing against the truth, but for the truth. For we are glad, when we are weak, and ye are strong: and this also we wish, even your perfection. Therefore I write these things being absent, lest being present I should use sharpness, according to the power which the Lord hath given me to edification, and not to destruction.

The occasion that produced this challenge to self-examination went back to the disturbance which had been created in Corinth by those who were maligning Paul and endeavoring to dispute and discredit the genuineness of his ministry. The finger of accusation was constantly upon Paul. They were demanding proofs of his power. Now he has suggested that they might turn their fingers upon themselves. Let them give whatever assurances they can that they are true and not false, redeemed and not reprobate. So he wrote, "Examine yourselves, whether ye be in the faith; prove your own selves. Know ye not your own selves, how that Jesus Christ is in you, except ye be reprobates?"

Three times in this one statement he has challenged them and us—"Examine yourselves . . . prove your own selves . . . know ye not your own selves . . ."

A. *The Purpose*—"Examine yourselves, whether ye be in the faith."

The examination which is suggested here is not that morbid inquiry which many persons engage in. They periodically pull out their feelings and expose them to the scrutiny of doubt. They never expect to be confirmed and are usually more gloomy afterward. This kind of self-examination is a form of spiritual disease. It is morbid spirituality. It is unholy and unhealthy.

There are legitimate moments of self-examination and proper methods of measuring one's self. The moment of self-examination is not the time of unbelief. "Do not dig up in unbelief what you have planted in faith." Growth is self-evident in any normal experience. Digging at the roots of your experience will retard growth and dwarf life.

B.   *The Process*—"Prove your own selves."

This means to test. It is the process of self-examination. You are not to test your feelings because they fluctuate and vary. You are to test your experience. The measuring instruments are the Spirit within and the Word without. These are the tests of who we are as well as what we do.

The Bible has many tests concerning what we do. Love is one: "We know that we have passed from death unto life, because we love the brethren" (I John 3:14). Overcoming is another: "For whatsoever is born of God overcometh the world: and this is the victory that overcometh the world, even our faith" (I John 5:4). Besides these, there are the tests of good works, kindness, purity, righteousness, worship, prayer and a host of additional evidences.

C.   *The Result*—"Know ye not your own selves, how that Jesus Christ is in you, except ye be reprobates?"

This is the result of the test and the accomplishment of the purpose—that we may know in and of ourselves. We do not need the assurance of ecclesiastical authorities.

Knowledge is the goal of Christian experience. What a tragedy if we could not know that we are Christians! Yet, vast numbers of professors do not know whether or not they are possessors. They have been told by misguided religious leaders that they should seek and strive and struggle and then when they die they will know.

We can know right now whether we are redeemed or reprobate, whether we are saved or lost, whether we are true or false. "Hereby know we that we dwell in him, and he in us, because he hath given us of his Spirit" (I John 4:13). "These things have I written unto you that believe on the name of the Son of God; that ye may know that ye have eternal life" (I John 5:13). Do you know?

You will notice that the challenge is for personal inspection: "Examine yourselves." We are not obliged to examine others, only ourselves. We are not answerable to God for anyone but ourselves.

It is much more interesting and exceedingly more comfortable and easy to examine someone else.

Two boys went into a dental office. One said boldly, "I have a tooth to be pulled. You need not give me any anaesthetic, just yank it out."

"All right, young man," said the dentist, "where's your tooth?"

The boy turned to his companion and said, "Willie, show him your tooth."

Most of us are very brave about the solution of other people's problems and the examination of other people's faith. We must be careful to note that the resultant knowledge of the test is the discovery of ourselves as either Christians or reprobates. Jesus Christ is in us or else the alternative is true.

A reprobate is not necessarily a scoundrel or a thief or an immoralist. A reprobate is one who is "not approved" or who cannot stand the test of approval. He is a still-born religionist.

There is another side to self-examination. It is not only to prove, but to improve. We can constantly improve ourselves by discovering flaws and eliminating faults.

There is the story of a man who kept his soul as clean as the best housewife keeps her house. Every night he swept out the dust and washed all the vessels of mind and soul. With this review came a renewal of life and that cleanness of cleansing by the Spirit of God that gave great peace.

The personal element which has been so pronounced and prominent in the writings of this Christian document to the Corinthians is now revealed in its best form. The man who has been so zealous for the spiritual improvement of the Christians at Corinth has also been severe and brutally frank in his censure and judgment, but upon all this he has drawn the veil of kindness and the covering of charity.

He did not find life perfect among the Corinthians. It was polluted by sin and torn by strife, but in spite of this it was enduring. He found for himself a way of life that could look trouble and disaster in the face and say, I am victor.

In these chapters we have followed Paul through every conceivable situation. We have seen him in prison, in floggings, in labors, in shipwreck and in such a variety of experiences that we marvel at his fortitude and endurance.

For this man it was a life that endured. It was not endurance in the sense in which we sometimes speak— endurance by reason of miserable patience. Paul endured because of a glorious perseverance. His endurance had the quality of an inner triumph; it was the success of a life within.

The life that endures is the life that is durable. It is the life of Christ in the life of the Christian. It has come from the fountainhead which is Christ. It has been tested on the anvil of experience. It has been proved through the centuries of time. It is yours for the taking and the living.

III. THE BENEDICTION OF FAREWELL (verses 11-14)

This conclusion begins with the word "finally." It is to be the last word, and, in many respects, the most important word. It must leave nothing in doubt or in a state of suspension. All that is to be said must be in the light of what has been said.

There is something sad about this "finally." It gives a feeling of regret that the epistle is to close. It is filled with expressions of truth which have grown out of the apostle's experiences. They are not professional literary phrases coined by a clever mind. They are not sayings gleaned from a dictionary of wit and wisdom. They are living truths forged out of the hot metal of experience.

However much we may regret this "finally, brethren" there is something about it that is satisfying as well as sad. We have been privileged to read in this autobiography eternal truths which will enrich our lives and increase our responsibilities.

There are three parts to this "finally, brethren."

A. *Final Counsel* (verse 11)

Finally, brethren, farewell. Be perfect, be of good comfort, be of one mind, live in peace; and the God of love and peace shall be with you.

This final counsel is a threefold challenge.

1. Be Perfected

Way suggests that this might mean "let there be a perfect reformation among you." It suggests a continuous growth in grace that will lead them on to increasing perfection. Paul did not pass a verbal wand of holiness over them to give them a negative perfection. He challenged them to Christian progress and perfection.

Here is a challenge for all of us. If we would indulge in a few serious moments of introspection, we would quickly see faults to be mended and ways to be amended. The decision for such amendment is the matter of a moment, but the accomplishment is a matter of development and growth.

2. Be Comforted

This does not mean comfort for sorrow but rather good cheer and encouragement in the attainment of the previously mentioned perfection.

Literally, it means that we are to stimulate one another. This shows a heart-interest in another's progress. It is the helpfulness of our encouragement instead of the hindrance of our criticism. Too many times we stifle instead of stimulate. We stifle another's sincere but halting efforts because we are too critical. It would add immeasurably to the efforts of others if we took a more charitable attitude and said, "God bless you, my friend."

3. Be United

This is the unison of unbroken communion. We observe the Lord's people being divided and scattered. It is an ancient trouble for it appeared in very violent form at Corinth. They were quarrelsome and contentious. Their divisions were not over great issues, but were the result of personal preferences and prejudices that brought estrangement.

Christians have been likened unto burning coals. If they are scattered far apart, they are easily extinguished, but when they are burning close together the heat of one preserves the heat of the other. Christians in communion strengthen each other and add a collective glow and fire that brightens and blesses the world. When they fall out and separate there are usually casualties among them. Some will grow cold and their lives will cease to glow with the usual warmth and fire.

B. *Final Salute* (verses 12-13)

Greet one another with an holy kiss. All the saints salute you.

The spirit of this act of Christian salute is more important than the letter of it. What was in that early day a common expression of brotherhood is not necessary in our day, but it is essential that we preserve the spirit of brotherhood. Let us forget the kiss but remember the kindness.

C. *Final Prayer* (verse 14)

The grace of the Lord Jesus Christ, and the love of God, and the communion of the Holy Ghost, be with you all. Amen.

The final prayer is not a petition but a benediction— that threefold benediction so common to our hearing. It sets forth the blessing of a triune God.

It imparts grace. Who of us can live a satisfying Christian experience without grace? It is that quality which covers our sins and compasses our weaknesses. It is as necessary to our existence as it is sufficient to our needs.

It imparts love. This is a quality of affection that softens our attitudes and inspires our purposes. It is something which brings God close to us. It is in fact, the practical realization of God, for He is love.

It imparts communion. This is the communion of fellowship. It is that communication of God's presence which keeps us from the feeling of lonesomeness that often creeps upon us in weary hours.

Here indeed is a practical manifestation of God in grace, in love and in communion.

Now we have finished. The apostle has laid down his pen and we are about to conclude our reading. We do it with regret, but it is hoped, with purpose. Let it be the purpose of pursuit in which we will pursue with determined consecration the goal of grace and the opportunities of experience that its truth sets forth.

There is much unexplored territory. There are many untouched treasures. There remains a challenge of grace for venturing faith. Let us be bold to follow and we shall be abundantly rewarded.

DATE DUE